Remembering
Lucy Maud Montgomery

ALEXANDRA HEILBRON

THE DUNDURN GROUP
TORONTO · OXFORD

Publisher: Anthony Hawke
Editor: Judith Turnbull
Design: Jennifer Scott
Printer: University of Toronto Press

Canadian Cataloguing in Publication Data

Heilbron, Alexandra
    Remembering Lucy Maud Montgomery

ISBN 1-55002-362-4

1. Montgomery, L. M. (Lucy Maud), 1874-1942. 2. Novelists, Canadian (English) — 20th century — Biography I. Title.

PS8526.O55Z768 2001   C813'.52   C2001-901940-8   PR9199.3.M6Z73 2001

1   2   3   4   5   05   04   03   02   01

 Canadä

THE CANADA COUNCIL | LE CONSEIL DES ARTS
FOR THE ARTS | DU CANADA
SINCE 1957 | DEPUIS 1957

ONTARIO ARTS COUNCIL
CONSEIL DES ARTS DE L'ONTARIO

We acknowledge the support of the **Canada Council for the Arts** and the **Ontario Arts Council** for our publishing program. We also acknowledge the financial support of the **Government of Canada** through the **Book Publishing Industry Development Program** and **The Association for the Export of Canadian Books**, and the **Government of Ontario** through the **Ontario Book Publishers Tax Credit** program.

Printed and bound in Canada.⊛
Printed on recycled paper.

www.dundurn.com

L.M. *Montgomery* is a trademark of the Heirs of L.M. Montgomery Inc.

Dundurn Press   Dundurn Press   Dundurn Press
8 Market Street   73 Lime Walk   2250 Military Road
Suite 200   Headington, Oxford,   Tonawanda NY
Toronto, Ontario, Canada England   U.S.A. 14150
M5E 1M6   OX3 7AD

Remembering
Lucy Maud Montgomery

This book is dedicated to my mother,
Jan Serlier Heilbron

Contents

Acknowledgments

This book wouldn't have been possible without the help of many people. Most importantly, the interviewees, who generously shared their time and memories, as well as George Campbell, Mary Beth Cavert, Brock and Sharon Clark, Harold Clark, Wilda Clark, Elaine Crawford, Gail and Bill Currie, Kathy Gastle, Judy Koshan, Stephan Lim, Anna MacDonald, Jennie and John Macneill, Norm McLeod, Robert Montgomery, Brenda Moore (née Harwood), Kathryn Morton, Mary Rubio, John Wallace, and especially my mother, Jan Serlier Heilbron.

Thanks to all of you!

Introduction

Most of L.M. Montgomery's books were so sunny and bright that her readers assumed that the author's life was exactly like that of the Anne of *Anne of Green Gables*, but when her journals were published, a darker side of L.M. Montgomery emerged. Naturally, this raised questions. Which L.M. Montgomery was the real Maud (as she preferred to be called) Montgomery? What was she *really* like?

Maud made an interesting assertion in an early volume of her journals. She claimed that when she was very young, she decided that no matter how difficult things were, no matter how she felt about certain people or aspects of her life, she would be cheerful and outgoing. She didn't want to darken other people's lives with her troubles. Consequently, she concluded, no one truly knew her. They only knew the optimistic, outgoing, and helpful L.M. Montgomery — she saved her problems for her journals.

Many entries were so dark and full of anguish that it is difficult to believe Maud could possibly have kept this part of her life to herself. While drowning in the sorrows revealed in her journal, could she really have presented herself as an upbeat, happy person to all who knew her?

I set about talking to people who had known her personally, to search out the answers. It gradually became apparent that just as Montgomery's books don't paint a true portrait of the author, neither do her journals. Perhaps this is because, as she openly admitted, she used her diaries largely to record her complaints. Not having a close friend in whom to confide her troubles, she wrote them down in order to get them off her chest. Naturally, some pleasant events were recorded, but considerable portions of the journals are filled with complaints, worries, and even nasty remarks. Writing in her journals was a catharsis for the often-troubled Maud.

Maud was an extremely busy person by choice, and as a minister's wife, a mother, and a world-famous author, she was under a lot of pressure. Some of this she brought on herself. Even though, for example, she had a maid to help with the cooking and housework, in her early married life Maud often insisted on planning menus and doing many of the chores herself. In addition, she ran several church groups, had members of the congregation over for visits or went to visit them, and set aside several hours each day for her writing. Maud also wrote in her journals and carried on a correspondence with pen-pals, fans, friends, and relatives. And she had two sons to look after — Chester, born in 1912, and Stuart, born in 1915.

When Maud's long-time pen-pal Ephraim Weber offered to write her biography after her death, she replied that she did not want him or anyone else to write her biography, because no one could ever give an accurate portrayal of another person. At least with respect to herself, Maud was absolutely right: no one truly knew her when she was alive. It has become clear that only certain aspects of her personality are portrayed in her books and journals. Only when we take in *all* the information — her novels, her journals, and the memories of the people who knew her — do we have as true a picture as possible of the real L.M. Montgomery. This book offers one more aspect, one more piece of the puzzle that was Maud. The following shows how she appeared to the people who knew her — the fans, friends, maids, Sunday school students, and family members.

Courtesy Robert Montgomery
Lucy Maud Montgomery
Heritage Museum

Chapter One
Maud, Beloved Aunt and Grandmother

L.M. Montgomery lived in Prince Edward Island from her birth in 1874 until 1911, when she married the Reverend Ewan Macdonald and moved to Ontario. Although only three of her twenty novels were written while she lived there, nineteen of her books took place in whole or in part on Prince Edward Island.

After her move to Ontario, Maud visited the Island as often as she could, first with her husband and their two boys, Chester and Stuart, and later, when her sons were grown and her husband was ill, by herself. Her last visit was in 1939. She had a number of close friends and relatives on the Island with whom she would stay. When Maud was a child, she loved to visit her four cousins,

L.M. Montgomery (seated far left with a cat in her lap) with cousins and friends, circa 1892.

Courtesy Prince Edward Island Public Archives and Records Office.

Clara, Stella, George, and Frederica Campbell, in Park Corner. Clara, Stella, and Frederica had grown up and moved away, but George was still living at the Campbell's farm in Park Corner with his wife, Ella, and their children. His mother, Maud's Aunt Annie, was also on hand.

The Campbells at Park Corner and the Webbs at Green Gables in Cavendish were among Maud's favourite people to visit during her vacations on the Island. Both sets of families were Maud's cousins, and the children called her "Aunt Maud." Because of their close relationship with their famous cousin, their memories differ from those of people in Ontario. They remember Aunt Maud as jolly — distinguished, but also full of fun, jokes, and laughter. This L.M. Montgomery — Maud of the Island — was unlike the L.M. Montgomery of anywhere else. Here she felt at home and free to be herself. Here she was down-to-earth, funny, and warm.

Georgie (Campbell) MacLeod

A bright, inquisitive child at the time her famous cousin came for frequent visits at the Campbell's farm in Park Corner, Georgie fondly remembers "Aunt Maud" as a loving, lively character who was full of stories and fun.

Georgie Campbell MacLeod was born in Park Corner, Prince Edward Island, in September of 1918. She was six weeks old when her father, George, and brother, Georgie, died during the Spanish flu epidemic that took thousands of lives around the world. The neighbours in Park Corner came by to bring food, but they were afraid to come in the house, fearing they might catch the deadly disease. All the Campbell children were sick with the flu, and the adults were in shock from the sudden deaths. To help take care of the sick, Maud's favourite cousin and kindred spirit, Frede Campbell, came from Montreal, while Maud arrived from Ontario. Maud decided that the baby girl, who was originally called Janet, should be renamed Georgie in honour of her deceased

Georgie at home in Prince Edward Island.

father and brother. Frede added MacFarlane as the child's middle name. It was her husband's last name, and just in case he didn't return from overseas, where he was fighting in the Great War, this was a way his name could live on.

Georgie MacFarlane Campbell MacLeod remains just as outgoing and vivacious today as she must have been when Maud was a frequent visitor to the Campbell home. Maud was fond of all the Campbell children and spoke warmly of them in her journals and letters. The Campbell children called her "Aunt Maud" at her request, while her sons, Chester and Stuart, called the Campbell children's mother "Aunt Ella." George Campbell, Georgie's father, and Maud were first cousins through the Macneill side, and their mother, Ella, was Maud's second cousin through the Montgomery side.

Before her visits to Park Corner, Maud would write to Ella and ask her not to tell anyone she was coming. She didn't want to see people until she was well rested, as she was tired out from her church and community work (not to mention her work as a writer). Despite that, she was often seen getting off the train in the small town of Kensington, and word of the world-renowned author's return to her homeland would spread quickly.

Georgie remembers those days clearly. "One day my mother said, *Maud, there's somebody coming to the front door and I don't know them. It must be for you.* Aunt Maud said, *Well, you didn't tell them now, Ella, I was coming?* And mother said, *No, I didn't, Maud. If it's for you, will you talk to them?* Aunt Maud said, *Oh, yes, I'll talk to them.*

"I can see her yet. She always wore a little apron and carried a little note-book with her at all times. When something would come up through the day that amused her, she'd stop right then and take the little notepad out and write it down. My mother would say, *That will appear in a book later on,* and sure enough, it did. When folks came to the door, they asked, *Is L.M. Montgomery here? Is it possible we could speak to her?* Mother said, *Oh, yes, come right on in.* So Aunt Maud would take off that little apron, which was a pattern she had before she went to talk to them. She was always so gracious and so nice.

"One thing I remember extremely well about Aunt Maud — she loved jewellery. She had all kinds of rings and necklaces on and a watch and a bracelet and earrings. One day I got up alongside of her on the chesterfield and I started looking at her rings. Aunt Maud said to me, *You like rings?* I answered, *Yes, I sure do.*

"She asked me, *Now which ring do you think would be the most expensive?* I checked them all out and of course, kid-like, I picked the one with the biggest, showiest stone. I said, *Well, that would be the most expensive, that would cost more.* She laughed and said, *That is a pretty ring. Guess where I got it.* Of course, at that time I hadn't travelled very much and I just wouldn't know. She said, *I got that at the five-and-ten-cent store, Woolworths.* I was old enough to realize, 'Oh, no, she wouldn't get it there,' so I laughed. She said, *Really, honestly, that's where I got that ring. If you'd have picked any other ring on my fingers, they're all good rings. But that one, it was so pretty I couldn't pass it up.*

"Another time I remember we had an old-fashioned parlour social. We don't have them anymore, but people would come from miles around and there'd be entertainment and a nice lunch and they'd pass the plate around. Anybody could put in that plate however much he or she wanted. It was sort of a money-making scheme. If they wanted to put in a quarter at that time, that would be pretty big money.

"So Aunt Maud was there at that time visiting when we had that parlour social. She had a pretty set of pearls on and during the course of the evening, the pearls let go and fell all over the living room floor, the same room Aunt Maud had been married in. They even rolled under the organ my mother had played Aunt Maud's wedding march on, that same organ. My best friend Helen and I got down, scrambling to pick up all the pearls. We searched and picked away and everybody thought, 'L.M. Montgomery's pearls, well, these must be priceless.' So we picked up all we could and we were still trying to find them. At last Aunt Maud whispered to us, *Never mind girls.*"

Georgie's friend Helen remembers that day. "She broke a string of beads and kids like us were scrambling to find them, but she finally told us, *Oh, they're only from Woolworths.* Which made her seem more like an average person. I was not very old when I met her and I was kind of in awe of her. It was just a treat to see her." Helen had read all of L.M. Montgomery's books prior to meeting her and so was well aware that Georgie's Aunt Maud was a famous author. Helen remembers that the parlour social was held in Maud's honour, to give people a chance to come and see her. "She always wore all kinds of jewellery — beads and earrings and rings and all sorts of things. She looked different from most of the people who would come to see her. No one would be dressed as elaborately as she would be. The Campbells always had a lot of visitors at that time and they were so busy at that house. The hospitality at that home was always wonderful. I met L.M. Montgomery's sons as well. They'd be chasing around. The Campbell kids were active, always playing and running and having a wonderful time. It was a great place to go for fun."

Georgie recalls stories of her older sister Amy's experiences with Aunt Maud. "Amy used to walk down to the beach with Aunt Maud. It was a sunny day and she'd carry a parasol that would be over Aunt Maud's head. At first, Amy looked forward to taking these trips with Aunt Maud, but as time went on, she found them very boring because Aunt Maud got sort of carried away. She would be dreaming away of what was going to come in those books. If Amy asked Aunt Maud a question, she would never hear. She was so engrossed in thinking about what was going in that book. So Amy couldn't wait to get down to the beach. Once they got down to the beach, Aunt Maud would say, *Well you can go and play and do what you want to*, so she'd be by herself. Aunt Maud loved peace and quiet and she would get ideas for her new book during those times on the beach.

"Another time, Aunt Maud was expecting very special company and she wanted everything to be just right. Her oldest boy, Chester, sometimes would cause a few problems with the kids; he liked to carry on and have a good time. He was that type — he liked to have a little extra excitement. Among the kids, it doesn't take too much. His brother Stuart was the quiet one. Anyway, on this particular day, Aunt Maud was worried because she wanted everything to go smoothly when these people came. They were special company. My grandmother said, *Amy will take care of all the kids and take them all back to the brook.* There was a brook back in our old place in Park Corner, where we used to catch trout.

"They went fishing, and suddenly Amy heard screams and roars out of Chester. In the process of fishing, he got the fish-hook into his posterior, rear end, whatever you want to call it [laughs]. And it was really embedded into the flesh. He was screaming; he'd fallen into the brook. So my sister thought, 'I'm in charge, what do I do here now?' Amy had been told — *Never leave wet clothes on, you could take pneumonia.* She decided the thing to do was to take Chester's clothes off. So she stripped Chester of his clothes but the fish-hook was still in his backside!

"Meanwhile, things were going grand at home, just as planned, when my grandmother heard the whoops and the screams coming from the brook. She looked out and she couldn't believe what she was seeing. Chester and Amy were leading the group. Amy was still holding the fishing rod and the line and the fish-hook, which was in Chester's rump. Needless to say, she was horrified. She ran out as fast as she could to get him into an outside building. She got some dry clothes for him and they had to take him to the nearest doctor, a good nine miles away, to get that fish-hook out. It wasn't too funny at the time, but it created quite a bit of laughter in later years. I wasn't very old at the time, but I heard my sister telling that story so many times that it keeps reviving all the time.

"Another time I remember at my old home in Park Corner, I heard Aunt Maud upstairs. I knew she was the only one that was up there, and I could hear her talking to herself. Well, as a kid, this amused me to no end. There she was up there talking to herself! So I crept up the stairs into the landing and I peeked at her through the rungs. She was up in the big hall and I was watching her and, oh, I was amused to death watching her. Finally she laughed right out loud and said, *That's just what I'll put down.* So she picked the little notepad out of her apron and started to write. With that, I moved on the landing and I guess the boards creaked. Aunt Maud looked down at me and said, *Georgie — how long have you been standing there?*" Georgie laughs at the memory. "I was only seven or eight and I thought, 'Oh, I've done something wrong,' and I hightailed it down those stairs. Not that she would have scolded me. Aunt Maud wasn't the type of person who would scold. She was a very lovable person.

Was she affectionate?

"Very much so [nodding emphatically]. Very much so. I remember as a child that when Aunt Maud would come to our place, we'd just love to see her coming because she always had gifts for us kids. Always. She was nice to have around.

"Aunt Maud was such a jolly person and it makes me sad today to hear these stories that she was blue and melancholy and all those things, but I guess that followed in later life. We didn't know that side of Aunt Maud when she came to our place. I can still hear her and my mother talking and reminiscing about yesteryear, about old courtships and the fun they had years ago, and they would laugh — the walls would almost vibrate with the laughter. That's something I remember very vividly about Aunt Maud. We always saw the side of her that loved fun and was very affectionate and we just loved to have her come home. It's as simple as that."

Did you see the boys again?

"Stuart used to come visit me. The last time was six weeks before he passed away and he was a great guy. We used to have a lot of fun together and he always called me 'Georgie Girl.' He loved fun, although he was very quiet. He was a doctor in Toronto, as you know. Every year he'd come home [to P.E.I.] and he'd say, *Georgie Girl, have you got another story for me.* And I'd generally have a story for Stuart and he'd laugh his head off."

How has knowing L.M. Montgomery affected your life?

"Yesterday [during a taping of a documentary for the CBC about Montgomery] there was a bunch of Japanese girls coming up the stairs [at the old home in Park Corner] and the interpreter heard me say, *That's the room I slept in when I lived here.* The interpreter said, *You slept in that room?* I said, *Yes, this was my home. This is where I was born.* At that time you didn't go to a hospital, you were born at home. Well, those Japanese girls got so excited. The interpreter said, *She slept in that room. This was her home.* Well, I can see one yet; she got up and she jumped up and down and said, *You?* [And I said,] *Yeah, me.* So with that, they wondered if they could have their pictures taken with me. By this time the CBC had gotten their cameras on us. One of them was so excited, she bowed to me, and she bowed and she bowed so it started to strike me as funny, so I started bowing back to her. Those girls were so excited; it was unbelievable because we grew up with Aunt Maud and she was just our aunt and we loved her and that was it. But all this excitement! I was on *Good Morning America* and I don't know how many calls I got that day. I got one from Florida right afterwards. I got one from Boston, one from Vancouver, three from Ontario, and of course, my sister from New Hampshire ... the calls just kept coming in. And then I got the loveliest letter from a lady who lives in South Carolina, and she wondered would it be possible to get a letter because she and her two daughters had read every book and they were just thrilled to death to watch the *Avonlea* series on television. So I wrote to her and included some pictures of the old home. But the enthusiasm, it's unbelievable!"

Amy (Campbell) Lambert

Born October 28, 1910, Amy is Georgie Campbell's older sister by ten years. At the age of eight months, Amy attended Maud and Ewan's 1911 wedding, held in the parlour of the Campbell home.

A youthful ninety years of age, Amy Campbell remains energetic and full of fun. When she and her sisters get together these days, they call it "the jolly racket." Growing up in the house at Park Corner, the children had enjoyed lively times, and when Maud came for a visit, she fit right in as a member of the family. "There were nine children in our family. Donald was the oldest, but only five survived. Georgie's the youngest. We call her the last of the litter," Amy explains with a laugh.

Amy's memories of Maud are from the late 1910s to the mid-1920s. "I didn't see Aunt Maud after I was sixteen because I was away, in training to be a nurse." The entire Macdonald family would come for a visit. "They would stay with us for probably two or three weeks at a time. I think Uncle Ewan had a month off."

Maud was already famous, but Amy doesn't remember strangers coming to the door asking to meet her. "I think it was more in my younger sisters Maud's or Georgie's era that strangers would come to visit, to see L.M. Montgomery. By and large, it was mostly family from Cavendish or Malpeque who would come to visit with Aunt Maud. She never really wanted people to know that she was there on vacation."

"She was fun," Amy remembers fondly when asked of her famous cousin. "And funny. Great sense of humour. She played with us. I didn't think of her as being a 'maître dame of the British Empire' [Maud was named a Companion to the Order of the British Empire in 1935] at that time.

"When I was about eight years old, I used to wipe the dishes and Aunt Maud would wash them. My grandmother told me that if she stopped washing the dishes and started to write or began to talk to herself, I was not to disturb her. You can imagine what that did to an eight-year-old then and there. I didn't like to do dishes anyway and I still don't like to do them. So I would

Amy (at left) with her sisters Maud and Georgie.

Courtesy Georgie MacLeod.

The Campbell home in Park Corner.

Photo by L.M. Montgomery, courtesy Prince Edward Island Public Archives and Records Office.

cool my heels there and wait for her to continue [washing the dishes]. I was privy to walking with Aunt Maud down to the shore. She had a parasol and I would carry that. Sometimes we communicated and most of the time we didn't. I just went with her and she wrote and talked to herself. We'd go down and sit on a rock and look at the ocean until it was time to come home. She talked to herself a lot and then she'd write. Her voice was very soft. I would say cultured."

Amy enjoyed the company of her cousins Chester and Stuart. "Chester was a year younger than me and I was put in charge of him. Chester was a little rambunctious but Stuart, who was my sister Maud's age, was the perfect one. I taught Chester to fish, but you've probably heard that story. We went and we dug the worms and cut the pole and put a string on it. We didn't have any fancy fly things, you know."

L.M. Montgomery helped keep the Campbell farm going when times became financially difficult after the death of Amy's father. Maud also helped in small ways, paying for niceties such as music lessons. "The organ lessons were a dollar per lesson," Amy recalls, "and when Aunt Maud came to visit us the next year, she heard me play the organ and told my mother she'd find a better place for her money. She didn't think I was a good candidate for music lessons. The only time I ever practised was when the dishes were being done. If somebody else would do the dishes, then I would practise."

So you weren't very fond of your lessons?

"No. I should have been, because everyone in the family was musical but me. I tried my hand at the ukulele as well, but it was a disaster. Later on, Aunt Maud financed my education. She paid for my nurse's training, and after I graduated I started paying her back when I received my first cheque. Well, she wrote me a letter in which she said I was the only one who ever paid her back. I guess everybody borrowed from her. She was the only one who had any money. My sister Maud went to Prince of Wales College and Aunt Maud financed her education because she was named for her. She was always very generous with us. Her books were sent to me, fresh from the publishers, signed "To Amy Campbell, Affectionately, Aunt Maud."

How did L.M. Montgomery dress?

"She was usually dressed up. Uncle Ewan was, too. He was a stodgy old Presbyterian minister. He used to wear his bowler hat and I can see him now with that pocket watch and fob. He'd come out with his striped grey pants and his jacket and he looked as if he was going to preach a sermon. I was in awe of him, maybe because they told me he was a minister."

How would you describe her physical appearance?

"She wore her hair up on top of her head. I've seen pictures that I can't identify with because in her later years she got heavy. I don't remember Aunt Maud as ever being heavy. She was always tall and slim. She had beautiful clothes. They would be hanging in the upstairs hall, so I would try them on from time to time. As a matter of fact, I went to school one day in one of her plaid skirts and I remember I had to roll it at the top and matched it with a pink blouse that had black beads all over it. Can you imagine what a hit I was?"

Did she know you wore her things?

"No, no, no, no, no. Now that was top secret. Well, I never heard her say anything. And I can't remember whether my mother caught up with me on that or not. But I know I used to have to wear buttoned boots and I hated them and I used to leave them under the bridge and walk to school with the rest of kids in my bare feet."

Why did you hate the boots?

"Oh, you had to button them and a lot of the other kids went to school in their bare feet in the summertime, you know."

In her journals, Maud wrote that when she was a child, she didn't want to wear buttoned boots to school but her grandmother made her.

"Well, maybe I inherited that then [laughs]."

When Maud and Ewan and the boys came to visit, did they go to church on Sundays?

"Oh, bless me, yes. They had a car and we still had a horse and buggy. It was great goings-on to be able to get a ride in that Chevrolet touring car. I can see it now, it was pretty fancy."

So you kids would get a ride to church in it.

"Oh, yes. That was top drawer."

The Montgomery side of Maud's family lived right across the road from your place. Do you remember her visiting them while she was staying with you?

"Yes, my mother used to go over. We are double first cousins with the Park Corner Montgomerys because my mother's mother was a Montgomery. And then we're related on the Macneill side. My grandmother Campbell was a Macneill and she was a sister of Aunt Maud's mother."

Did Maud tell you kids stories? Or read to you?

"Aunt Frede was the one who used to read to us. That was my father's sister, who was my Aunt Maud's kindred spirit — her very best friend. Aunt Maud, when she visited, was invited out a lot. I think the adults were glad to get rid of us children after supper. It was her vacation time, after all."

Which room did she stay in?

"Uncle Ewan and Aunt Maud had the first room on the left as you go in the door towards the parlour. The spare room. She always slept there when she visited. The boys stayed in the other side of the house — we called it the back bedroom. Chester used to sleep upstairs some of the time at the head of the stairs. It was a big family; we were sleeping double. There were no twin beds; we slept double when company came."

Did Maud ever help with the baking?

"She would help my mother when we had company. We had a maid at that time because we had so many children. Aunt Maud liked to help. She didn't just sit. She was a very, very good cook."

Did she have a favourite food?

"She liked all food [laughs]. She and Aunt Frede used to talk about some kind of a ham and to this day, I really never knew what it was, exactly. Beef ham. They used to have snacks after they got us all in bed. I've often wondered what the beef ham was."

The Campbell home in Park Corner, now known as the Anne of Green Gables Museum at Silver Bush, is open to the public. Operated by George Campbell (Amy and Georgie's nephew), it is still furnished as it was when Maud was a frequent visitor; it even has the organ that Ella (Amy and Georgie's mother) played at Maud's wedding. The house also contains items from Maud's own home in Cavendish. When her grandmother died in 1911, Maud went to stay with the Campbells for several months prior to her marriage to the Reverend Ewan Macdonald. She brought with her furnishings from her old home, including her wall mirror and the famous bookcase with the glass panes in which she envisioned her two imaginary childhood friends, Katie Maurice and Lucy Gray. She later incorporated the bookcase and the imaginary friends into *Anne of Green Gables*. Throughout her childhood years, and later in her adulthood, Maud enjoyed many good times with her merry Campbell cousins in their Park Corner home.

Roma (Montgomery) Campbell

Roma Montgomery was thirteen years old the last time Maud visited the Island, in 1939. Her father, Heath Montgomery, was L.M. Montgomery's first cousin, and Maud, while staying at the Campbell farm across the road from the Montgomery homestead, would come over and visit the Montgomery family as well.

"She used to get my brother Jim and me to go down to the beach with her and get driftwood for the fireplace because the salt in the driftwood would make different-coloured flames. I remember her coming to visit my parents (Heath and Mary Ella Montgomery), because she was my father's first cousin. I was quite young then and my father had innumerable cousins, so she was really just another cousin coming to visit. I remember her as being very nicely dressed and she was sort of a sophisticated lady. As children, that's how we saw her. She was always quite friendly with the children.

"She always carried a notebook with her and when something would come to her mind she would jot it down. My father used to talk about something that

Roma Montgomery Campbell.

happened and she would take that and change the names and have it in her books. I can remember her writing little things that my parents were talking to her about and she'd make a note of it in her notebook, things that happened in the family and she used that notebook for ideas for her books.

"One thing I do remember, in 1935 I believe it was, she was given the Order of the British Empire and I can remember how proud she was in showing that. She brought it with her when she came to visit. She was so proud of that honour.

"She usually stayed over at the Campbell's farm, but she would spend a day or so at our place and my mother would have her over for meals. Her sons used to come when they were younger. I heard my mother mention them but I didn't really know them. I had seen her husband but usually she came by herself for a visit with us as far as I can remember and she and my dad would sit and reminisce.

"I can't remember what I called her. I didn't call her Aunt Maud. My father called her Maud, but some people called her Lucy Maud."

In 1928, when Roma was two years old, Maud gave a rare Australian edition of *Emily's Quest* to the little girl with the inscription "To Roma, with best wishes from her cousin L.M. Montgomery Macdonald 1928."

Roma believes that L.M. Montgomery's journals should have been either kept private or published later. "There are a lot of her innermost thoughts in them. Maybe fifty or seventy years down the road it would have been a differ-

Roma as a child with her neighbour, Ella Campbell.

Courtesy Robert Montgomery.

ent thing, but it was upsetting for the families of some of the people she wrote the comments about. It would have been better if some of her comments had been edited." She believes that Maud had been in a bad mood when she wrote many of these negative remarks and that the next day, feeling better, she might have felt entirely different about things.

Roma holds a place on the board of the L.M. Montgomery Birthplace in New London. She lives halfway between the L.M. Montgomery Birthplace and her own birthplace, the Montgomery homestead in Park Corner. Roma's younger brother Robert runs the Montgomery homestead, known to tourists as the L.M. Montgomery Heritage Museum. It is an elegant, large home with a winding footpath leading right back to the ocean. Maud stayed at the Montgomery homestead several times while a child, visiting her grandparents, and slept in the small room at the front of the house. The home has been kept exactly the way it was in those days, with all the same furnishings, including the green-spotted china dog Magog, who figured so prominently in the Anne books as well as in Maud's journals.

Keith Webb

Keith Webb grew up at Green Gables, the farm depicted by L.M. Montgomery in Anne of Green Gables, *and he recalls his famous cousin's frequent visits to his home.*

Keith Webb knew L.M. Montgomery, or Aunt Maud, as he and his sisters called her, from the day he was born — December 8, 1909. At the time, Maud lived with her grandmother in Cavendish, just across the road from his family's home, Green Gables, and she would often visit. His mother, Myrtle Macneill Webb, was Maud's third cousin and the two women were close friends.

Anne of Green Gables was published in 1908, and the Webbs' home was instantly recognized as the setting for the book. By the time Keith Webb was born a year later, their home had become famous thanks to the enormous popularity of *Anne of Green Gables*, and from that time on, it was known as Green Gables.

Keith's mother, Myrtle Webb, moved to Cavendish in 1894 when she was eleven years old. She lived at Green Gables with David and Margaret Macneill, a brother and sister who were her great uncle and aunt. In her teens, Myrtle befriended Maud, who had been away teaching at various schools. The two young women became close friends, sharing not only a love of nature but also the experience of living with older relatives who had taken them in and raised them. "Aunt Maud always told us that the character of Anne was a combination of her own life and my mother's life," Keith recalls. When Myrtle married

Keith Webb

Ernest Webb in 1905, they lived at Green Gables and helped Margaret and David Macneill run the hundred-acre farm.

Maud had a special feeling for Green Gables, where she'd spent so many hours walking down Lover's Lane and through the surrounding woods. Because of her close friendship with Myrtle, she had an open invitation to stay with the Webbs while in P.E.I. on vacation. She was always excited to be back at Green Gables, where she'd spent so many happy times growing up. Maud always stayed in the Webbs' guest room, opposite the one now known as "Anne's room." Although Ewan would accompany Maud when she went to Green Gables, he would stay for just a short time and then go and visit his family, who were still living on the Island. Maud would remain in Cavendish with the two boys. "She used to stay sometimes two or three weeks with us, she and the two boys," Keith says. He recalls seeing Ewan fill in as guest preacher at the Cavendish church while he was there on visits, but doesn't remember much more about him.

What was Maud like?

"Oh, I always said, kind of sophisticated [laughs]. You know what I mean? She seemed as if she thought she was a little better than the rest of us. I don't think she really thought that, she just kind of gave you that impression. Of course, she *was* a little more sophisticated. Yet she thought nothing of coming to the back field with you to get the cows, bring them in [through Lover's Lane] for milking. You know, she was just an ordinary woman. And she thought nothing about sitting down at the farm table in the kitchen with the farm help in their overalls."

Did she help milk?

"No, she'd never help milk, but she'd come to the barn with us. She liked to watch us give milk to the cats. They'd sit up on their hind legs and we'd squirt milk into their mouths."

Was she friendly?

"Oh, yeah. Yeah. She'd visit around town."

Did she laugh a lot?

"Not a lot, no."

Maud loved to wander on the beach and splash about in the water, and the five Webb children — Marion, Keith, Anita, Lorraine, and Pauline — would all go with her and her two boys. "We took her to the beach with a truck wagon, pulled by a team of horses. A truck wagon is a wagon used for hauling in hay and general purpose around the farm, before there were any tractors. She'd climb up into the truck wagon and we'd go to the beach, gather up wood through the day and have a bonfire there at night."

L.M. Montgomery as
Keith remembers her.

*Courtesy Prince Edward
Island Public Archives and
Records Office.*

What were her boys like?

"Chester was big and rough. One time, when he was about twelve, she forbade him to get into mother's strawberry patch. We kept boarders [tourists] in the summer and had a big patch of strawberries so we would have enough to serve to the guests. Well, right after dinner that night, he was missing. His mother looked around and back through Lover's Lane, calling him. Finally he showed up. He'd eaten all he could, and he had a pair of tight khaki shorts on and he'd filled the pockets full of strawberries. Juice was running down both legs. Aunt Maud always carried a black stick to punish the boys. She got some use out of it that night [laughs]. She was a good mother. Strict, but real good."

Did Maud ever help with the baking?

"One thing I do remember. It was Friday and we had a bunch of men there to help do the threshing. Our help was mostly French Catholics, so we always had fish on Friday. Aunt Maud was helping take up the mackerel for dinner. She had a big scoop that she was using to take the pieces of mackerel out of the boiling water, to put on a plate, when a piece slid off the scoop and hit one of the cats on the head. Scalded it. We had to do away with the cat. That really broke her heart. She was trying to help and it fell on a cat's head. Just a small cat. That hurt her pretty bad. That was one thing I never forgot, because she was so upset by it."

Mr. Webb has a guidebook of Prince Edward Island that contains several pages of colour images of Green Gables, including photos depicting the inside of the house as it is today. The photos bring back memories. "Mother used to cook on that stove. And that [pointing to another photo] was the author's typewriter. She told us that her publishers refused to accept any more handwritten manuscripts from her, so she got a typewriter — they had trouble reading her handwriting."

In fact, at least one error was made in an early L.M. Montgomery book when she was still writing manuscripts by hand — *Kilmeny of the Orchard*. The title of the first chapter was mistakenly interpreted by the printer as "The Thoughts of South." Later editions ran the corrected version — "The Thoughts of Youth."

Keith Webb looks at a photo of huge birches at the north side of Green Gables. "My sister Anita and I planted those trees at the side of the house over seventy years ago. Aunt Maud loved birches and she asked us to plant some there. Everybody told us they wouldn't grow, but they did," he notes with satisfaction.

A view of Green Gables showing the barn and other outbuildings that were torn down when Green Gables became a tourist attraction.

Photo by L.M. Montgomery, courtesy Prince Edward Island Public Archives and Records Office.

What kind of lighting did you have in the house?

"Oil lamps. Kerosene. The last few years I was there we had the big gas lanterns. And we milked the cows by hand. There was no electricity, you see."

Was there an outhouse?

"Yep."

Where was it?

"Just before Lover's Lane, at the opening of Lover's Lane."

Did you ever visit Maud in Ontario?

"No, but my sister Marion went up with her and stayed awhile, and a bit later on she married Murray Laird [a Norval resident] and settled down in Norval, Ontario."

Keith Webb's first wife, Margaret, died at the age of twenty-eight, leaving him with two small daughters. The funeral was held on his thirty-first birthday, December 8, 1940. His sister Anita, who was working as Montgomery's house-keeper in Toronto at the time, arranged to take a month off to help her brother through that difficult time.

With most of his family now living in Ontario, Mr. Webb decided to take his two daughters and move there as well. He worked for awhile as a farmhand before opening his own florist shop in Norval. In 1944 he married Ethel Swindlehurst, a friend of his sister Anita.

In the late thirties, the Government of Canada decided that Green Gables should be part of the Prince Edward Island National Park. Ernest Webb was given $6,000 for his farm and was allowed to remain there as park warden until he reached the age of sixty-five, at which time he was required to retire. On Ernest's retirement, he and Myrtle moved to another home in Cavendish. The government, meanwhile, tore down the Green Gables barn and driving shed as well as all the other outbuildings. In the late 1990s, a decision was made to restore them back to the way they were when *Anne of Green Gables* was written. Because Keith Webb was the person who could best remember the buildings, he was consulted about what the buildings had looked like and where they had been situated. Among other details, he was asked about the flooring that had been used; the style of hinges on the doors as well as the precise number of hinges and pegs; the direction that the doors opened; and the number of panes of glass in the windows. According to Keith, the house itself has been preserved pretty much the same way it was when he lived there.

Although Keith Webb has never read L.M. Montgomery's books, he is very proud of her accomplishments. He has a photograph of Maud, taken in her later years; she is wearing a white hat and looks very distinguished. "I remember her like that, more than anything else. With that hat. She was a very likeable person."

Marion (Webb) Laird

Marion first met Maud when she was her neighbour in Cavendish; later she knew Maud as a frequent visitor to her parents' home, Green Gables, and later still as a neighbour in Norval, Ontario. Having no daughters of her own, Maud felt a special affinity for Marion.

Marion Laird, née Webb, is Keith Webb's older sister by two years. When she was born on June 6, 1907, her mother, Myrtle Macneill Webb, was Maud Montgomery's closest friend in Cavendish. Maud spent a lot of time at their farm, either visiting with the Macneills/Webbs or enjoying solitary walks through the woods that surrounded the place. A pretty little blond girl with a sweet disposition, Marion was considered by Maud to be her special pet.

Marion's bedroom in the Green Gables house was the one now known as "Anne's Room." Located just at the top of the stairs, the tiny room overlooks the front yard and the old apple tree. Only four years old when Maud moved away to Ontario, Marion remembers Maud best from her frequent visits to Prince Edward Island.

What's your earliest memory of L.M. Montgomery?

"Well that's a way back when, isn't it? I was just a little girl when she came to our place every summer for a week or ten days."

How did she arrive at Green Gables?

"We met her at the train station in a horse and carriage."

What was Maud like? Did she have you on her lap, hug you?

Marion Webb Laird.

"Not really, no. But she had no girls of her own, just two boys. I guess she had always wanted a little girl, so I fitted in all right. I was very fond of her. Aunt Maud always had stories to tell about different people she knew. She loved our farm, Green Gables, and the lane that was called Lover's Lane and the Haunted Woods. Aunt Maud loved wandering back through the bush. She loved going off by herself, actually. We had a hundred acres on our farm and there was quite a lot of bush and pasture of course, and the fields for the cows and the cattle had made these paths through the woods and she liked exploring."

What did you like best about Aunt Maud?

"Her laughter. Simple little things that she found amusing. People amused her very much. The different characters that were around back in the old days. I liked her stories and the way she told them. She didn't just sit there and talk. Aunt Maud talked with her hands, if you know what I mean. She was quite active and animated."

Do you remember her sons?

"I remember her sons very well. The younger one, Stuart, was bright and fit and ready for anything, and the older one, Chester, was 'Oh, do I *have* to do that today, Mother?' [Laughs.] Do you know what I mean? I don't know how to describe him. A bit awkward."

Were they well behaved?

"Well, they were boys, real boys, and they were full of mischief when they were growing up, but as they grew up, yes, Stuart especially. He was very bright, very mannerly."

Would you say she was strict with them?

"Yes, she was."

How did she discipline them?

"Well, I can remember a strap being used. That was when they were younger. As they grew older, they behaved better. There was a black stick as well. They got spanked with that occasionally or on their hands. But they were as different from each other as Aunt Maud and her husband were."

Do you remember Reverend Macdonald?

"Oh, yes. He was just as fond of the Island as she was, really. Some of his people were still living there."

What was he like? Was he a warm person?

"I would say so. He was a tease — that's putting it mildly. But we all liked him and he and Grandpa [David Macneill] had great times telling stories to each other of the days gone by."

What was Maud's relationship with Margaret and David Macneill?

"She respected them. They were quite elderly. The farm was their home, and when my mother and dad were married, Aunt Margaret and Uncle David asked them to come stay with them and look after them and the farm. That's how I happened to be born at Green Gables. I looked after Aunt Margaret — she was blind. She went around the house with her hands out in front of her. She was very sarcastic, and Uncle David was just the opposite. He was so gentle, so kind. Spoiled us children. Thought nothing was too good for us. Aunt Margaret was just the opposite [wags her finger] — *You shouldn't let them do that!* If you know what I mean [laughs]. Uncle David's room was the one downstairs, the one they call 'Matthew's room.'"

How did you get to school?

"Walked through the woods. It really wasn't far, but to go around by the highway, it was four times farther so we went through the woods. It would have been a cow path, I guess. The cattle went down for a drink in the brook and then up to the pasture. It took me a while to get acquainted at school. I was afraid of the boys. There were two or three other girls that I knew before I went to school, and for a while I wouldn't go unless I was sure that Leeta and Nellie were there. They were a little bit older than I was. There was a French hired man, called Tannis for short, and his daughter also watched over me."

Why was the roof of Green Gables raised over the kitchen? Do you remember when that happened?

The Haunted Woods, "Green Gables", Cavendish, Prince Edward Island, National Park 54

A vintage postcard of "The Haunted Woods" at Green Gables.

"Oh, yes. There were carpenters around. There were also neighbours who helped out, and my father was a good carpenter himself. It was because of the family growing. There were five children by the time my youngest sister, Pauline, was born."

Did you have indoor plumbing?

"No [laughs]. We had a pump and we heated the water on the stove."

What kind of lighting did you have?

"Oil lamps. When you went down cellar you had to carry a lantern."

What did you keep down there?

"Potatoes, carrots, turnips, all kinds of vegetables. It was always cool down there."

Were those grown right on the farm?

"Oh, yes. Certainly. We also had corn, and the grain was sold. We grew wheat. Good fields of wheat and potatoes."

Did you help gather them up?

"Sure. That's part of growing up on a farm."

Have you been back to it?

"Oh, yes, but it was all changed. When the golf course was built, the farm was completely changed. Lover's Lane actually continued much further originally, but that was all remodelled because of the fairways."

Maud liked taking photographs. Did she often carry a camera?

"Not often, but there were parts of the farm that she wanted to remember. There was a nice little lake on the farm that ran down to the beach and she loved that part of it. We had quite a nice woods. Mostly spruce and elm and

A back view of Green Gables.

Photo by L.M. Montgomery, courtesy Prince Edward Island Public Archives and Records Office.

birch. I remember she carried a notebook and would practise her speedwriting. The faster she could write, asking different questions, the better because she had to put it down fast."

What kinds of questions did she ask?

"Oh, about people. The older people in the vicinity. What they were doing and how they were. She was very much concerned with whether they were being taken care of."

How did Maud look, physically?

"She had very fine features. She was very particular about her clothes. They had to be just right. She always looked like a well-dressed lady."

Did you read her books?

"Of course, dear, I read them all. Yes."

Did she give you copies?

"Oh, yes."

Did you talk with her about them?

"[Pause.] We laughed about them. Some of her funny stories, the amusing things that happened with our older folk, our neighbours."

Do you remember if she did any handiwork?

"Oh, yes. She did crocheting and knitting. She might have done tatting too, I'm not sure."

What sorts of things did she make?

"Well, she crocheted a lace centrepiece for our table."

In August 1927, after vacationing at Green Gables, Maud brought Marion back to Norval with her for a two-month visit. While there, Marion went with the Macdonalds to spots such as the Canadian National Exhibition in Toronto, and Niagara Falls. During her visit in Norval, Marion met Murray Laird. The two young people visited back and forth between Norval and Prince Edward Island, and were eventually married on October 4, 1934, at the Norval manse.

Was Reverend Macdonald the minister at your wedding?

"Yes, he was the minister. And Aunt Maud served lunch after the wedding ceremony."

Marion lived in Norval after her wedding, not far from Maud, and attended the Presbyterian church where Reverend Macdonald served as minister. "Aunt Maud had never had a daughter and, well, just took me under her wing, I guess. She was certainly as kind as any mother could be."

Lorraine (Webb) Wright

Lorraine Webb grew up at Green Gables as the fourth of five children. In the late 1930s, Lorraine taught school in Cavendish for three years. Then, in 1940, during the Second World War, she went to Ottawa to work in the naval service headquarters as a code and cipher clerk. She was married in 1944. Lorraine had planned to have her wedding on the front lawn of her childhood home, but instead was married in the church, since a golf tournament had been scheduled at Green Gables for that day.

"I was born May 28, 1917. I certainly remember Aunt Maud and we always looked forward to her visits and her stories and walking back through the woods with her, back of Lover's Lane and so on. She loved Lover's Lane and the shore especially.

"When my family lived at Green Gables, there was a hen house and a granary and a machine shed. My chores included bringing in the cows and milking them, too. We had hens and geese and pigs and horses. The driveway we had then was west of the barns. The road back to Lover's Lane would go straight back from the laneway. We just loved the woods. All of us did. It was nice and quiet and peaceful. We'd play in the woods, building playhouses. We carried branches for ever so far. My mother and sister would come and have afternoon tea with the old broken cups. That was down in the Haunted Woods across the brook.

"We had so many visitors every summer. Hundreds of people would visit the house every day. They usually came just as we were sitting down for a meal. They'd ask weird questions. It was all so real to them. They didn't realize the story was fictional. Some of them thought mother was Anne and that made her very annoyed. We also had a small tearoom at the house. The golf course was open at that time and we served light lunches and we also had copies of the L.M. Montgomery books for sale.

"Aunt Maud liked to dress well. She loved hats. She was a wonderful story-teller. Some of the neighbours would come in and they would swap stories. She would tell stories of some of the characters who lived in the community. Every community has unique characters. I remember the night she spoke to our Young People's group down at the shore and told about the *Marco Polo* [a ship] going down there, right off that very shore, when she was a small girl. I would have been about thirteen at the time she told us that story.

"She used to send us a box of books at Christmas. Her publishers would give her books and she'd send them on to us. We were all avid readers. She usually brought us little gifts when she came to visit. A bit of jewellery or something

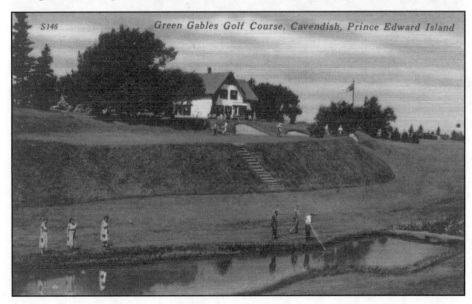

A vintage postcard of Green Gables as it was in the 1940s.

that kids would like. Mother and Dad always received a copy of her latest book. We read all of them. I've read them all several times."

Lorraine remembers that Montgomery had a special affinity for Marion, Lorraine's eldest sister. "I think Marion was her favourite. She was very fond of Marion."

"Aunt Maud divided up her holidays because she had other friends that she always stayed with. Maybe she'd stay with us for a week. Her husband sometimes came with her, but he never stayed at our farm. He was from the Island as well, so I think he went to visit his family and friends. I remember one year in particular when their boys were there. They were both older than I was. We enjoyed going to the shore. I remember Stuart walking the ridge pole of the barn. It was a fairly high barn. He was very active. He was a gymnast when he got a little older. Aunt Maud was very fond of her children."

Postcard from the 1940s of Green Gables. You can see where the grass has been removed to create a sand trap for the golf course.

"Green Gables", Cavendish, Prince Edward Island National Park.

Luella (Macdonald) Veijalainen

Only four of L.M. Montgomery's seven grandchildren are biologically related to her, and all four are Chester's offspring from his two marriages, first to Luella Reid and then to Ida Birrell. Of Chester's children, only the two from his first marriage were born while L.M. Montgomery was alive — Luella and her younger brother, Cameron. Maud's son Stuart and his wife, Ruth (Steele), had children by adoption, as did David, Chester's son from his second marriage. Catherine, David's sister, has never had children. Luella's daughter, Karem, then, is L.M. Montgomery's only surviving biologically related great-grandchild, and Karem's son, Erik John, born on April 25, 1996, the only great-great-grandchild. Luella Macdonald Veijalainen, Maud's first-born grandchild, is a lively, vibrant, busy person.

What comes to mind when you think about your grandmother?

"I remember my grandmother as just an older person, and she had that older-age palsy kind of thing, the shaking hands. It was probably the effects of veronal, but I don't think she was using those things all the time. I always called her Donny. That was what she wanted me to call her, not 'Grandmother.' I didn't think about it at the time, but I realized later it was a short form for Macdonald.

"She always made sure I had books to read. A book publisher from Australia contacted her for her opinion on some children's books. She thought, 'What better person to criticize children's books than a child.' I remember one vividly, it was *Blinky Bill* — about a koala bear. It was fantastic. Another one was *People*

L.M. Montgomery
proudly holds her
first grandchild, Luella,
born May 17, 1934.

*Courtesy Luella
Macdonald Veijalainen.*

of the Dark, a story about abo-
rigines. They stuck in my
head. There were other ones,
but these two I remember.

"Another thing about
her, she always gave gifts that
would last. I have a little car-
nival glass plate that she gave
me and I still use it for serving
cookies. Also, a framed picture of Lover's Lane. They
were both Christmas pres-
ents, something that you
keep, not something you just
play with and get tired of."

**Do you remember her hold-
ing you on her lap, or taking
you by the hand?**

"Well, I'm sure she did stuff
like that, I just don't remem-
ber. To, me, she was just my grandmother. I would say that what I remember
is the house. I remember the yard. The graveyard of cats. [Maud buried her
cats in the backyard of the Toronto home, under rocks especially brought
from Prince Edward Island.] My brother, who's two years younger than I am,
disappeared once while we were there and they couldn't find him. He
climbed out the window and was on the little roof over the front door."

Did you live there or were you visiting?

"We'd stay overnight, a weekend visit or something like that."

Where did you live?

"We started out in Toronto and then after I was born, we couldn't be in that apartment anymore. So we went back to my mother's parents' farm. My dad would come home on the weekends from Osgoode [the school where he was studying in Toronto]."

What was your grandmother's usual demeanor?

"I really can't remember. The thing is, to me, she wasn't any different than my mother. Well, she was older, of course. But that's just the way we were. We weren't hanging from the chandeliers back then. We were, shall we say, 'the Scottish type.' Even if you're not living there, in Scotland."

In several biographies of L.M. Montgomery, Maud's Macneill grandparents, the ones who raised her, are often described as "strict" and "taciturn," and reference is made to how difficult it must have been for a sensitive child to be brought up by such people. It has also been said that Maud sacrificed quite a lot to stay at home in Cavendish with her Grandmother Macneill until the old lady's death. What isn't taken into account are the sacrifices the Macneill grandparents made for Maud, taking her in after her mother (their daughter) died and raising her, despite the fact that they were getting on in age.

"It makes me mad when I read something that's said about her 'stern grandparents.' That's what people were like then! Her grandparents weren't any different from anyone else. That's just the way people were. You acted the way you were supposed to. Of course, back in those days, too, if you were the last child left in the home, you were responsible for looking after the older person. That's the way things were done."

Did you have any idea when you were small that your grandmother was a famous person?

"Well, I read very early. I loved reading. So I was aware quite early on."

Do you have a favourite book by her?

"I liked them, but I haven't read every darn book that she wrote. I just didn't come across a whole lot of them. My mum bought me some. I liked *Anne*, and that melodramatic *Kilmeny of the Orchard*. When I was a kid, I loved that one. I would have probably been in grade seven or eight when I read it. In later years, I came across *A Tangled Web*. I liked that, it was good. There were different ones that I liked, for certain reasons."

How did she dress in daily life?

"Well, just cotton dresses, like everybody else. Housedresses. That was the day of the housedress and an apron. Some dresses that you see on women now in the summertime, going somewhere, that was a housedress when I was a kid. The type of things that you'd be wearing to wash dishes. And you'd have an apron on. If you suddenly went running down the street, you'd quickly take the apron off. Now instead of housedresses, people wear jeans."

Luella's father, Chester, married Luella Reid in 1933, and Luella Agnes Josephine Macdonald was their first child, born May 17, 1934. They had another child, Cameron Craig Stuart, born April 29, 1936 (Cameron died in December 1999), but a few years later, Chester and Luella divorced. "My brother and myself were the only two grandchildren my grandmother knew. And then my dad got married again. She really was upset when all that happened. And of course, I don't remember at the time, but obviously she sided with my mother."

Did your father visit you and your brother after the divorce?

"I only saw him twice. Those were the terms of the agreement. It was a long time ago and they thought, in their misguided way, that we would be better off if we didn't see the other half, that we'd be getting more upset or something.

"I would have been seven when the split came, and when I was eleven, my dad wanted to set up a visit. He kept tabs on us; he knew what we were doing all the time. So my mum took us to the Royal Ontario Museum in Toronto and we looked around first, then she sat us on a bench at the end of a long corridor and said, *Now you sit there and don't you move.* Then she went to the other end of the corridor and watched until she saw my dad arrive near us, and then she left.

"We went out to dinner, to the Ontario Club. It was roast beef dinner, I remember that. But what else did you get back then? So we had roast beef dinner and then we went to the Royal Alexandra Theatre and saw Clarence Day's play *Life with Father.* I remember that play well — someone said 'damn' on the stage and I was excited because he swore on stage! I never forgot it! [Laughs.] There wasn't too much of that except for the famous line from *Gone with the Wind.* So this 'damn' on the stage, I liked that."

What was it like to see your father after all that time? Was it like seeing a stranger?

"No, I enjoyed that day. I didn't feel uncomfortable or anything like that. He was good with kids. And of course, the divorce was long since, so I wasn't really thinking of that, I wasn't thinking, 'Are we going to get back together?'

"The next time I saw him I was eighteen. I was working up at Windermere House in Muskoka. He went to visit my mother, just presented himself at the door. And my mother said, *Oh, I suppose you want to see the kids.* I think my brother had found him sometime; he was interested in seeing him. So she gave my father my address at Windermere's. He wrote me a letter and I was really anxious to see him. We used to get hours off — I think now you get one or two days off, but you only got hours back then. So he came and I was all dressed up in a candy-striped dress and a little peter pan collar and my hair was all done — I'd had a new perm. I hadn't seen him for a while. I was dressed up; you didn't throw on jeans back in those days to go somewhere.

"I trained for nursing at Toronto General. When I was a student, something occurred [regarding my father] and I heard it over the radio and this was long since my grandmother died so it really made me mad when I heard [someone on the radio mention L.M. Montgomery in reference to Chester being disbarred] — and I thought, 'What's that got to do with my grandmother? She's already long dead.' He [Chester] was a lawyer, remember, but anyway, he lost his licence over that. Over a legal thing. And I thought, 'Whatever did they mention that for? It's got nothing to do with my grandmother.'" Luella was so irritated by the event that some time later, when Chester called her after the birth of her first son, Lauri, she cut the phone conversation short. "I said, *I'll send you a picture,* and *click* [hung up]."

Although Chester and his new wife had two children, Luella didn't see her half-siblings for many years. While attending an unveiling of a portrait of L.M. Montgomery in Uxbridge, Luella saw a man across the room and thought that he looked a bit like her brother.

"It turned out that he was looking at me, saying to his wife, *She looks like my sister.* We weren't introduced until later. That's the first time I met David. It was funny because we were going camping down east, my husband, Antti, and the two kids and I, and David and his wife said, *Well, we're going down too!* So we camped together at Park Corner. Actually, my husband and kids slept in the tent and I slept in a room in the Campbell house [now the Anne of Green Gables Museum at Silverbush]. I slept under the crazy quilt that my grandmother made, the one that's now in the glass case there."

Luella worked as a registered nurse for many years before retiring. She and Antti (pronounced Andy) had three children, two boys and a girl. John Erik, the middle child, was hit by a car while delivering newspapers and killed. He was only twelve years old. "That was a sad situation. He was hit by a neighbour whose own kid was in the car, who was a friend of my daughter's.

December 14th. It was dusk when he was coming home and he drove for a living. Apparently he'd said a couple of days before to his wife, *You know, in all these years I've been driving for a living, I've never had an accident.* Then he said, *And when I do, it'll probably be a doozie.* He said that two days before. And it was just a little bit of dusk and he was coming up this little rise and Erik just went across the road."

Luella's eldest son, Lauri Montgomery, died several years ago due to an illness, and her husband a few years before that. Despite the tragedies in her life, Luella has remained active and involved in the community. As a volunteer for the Big Sisters Organization, she has been a Big Sister for two girls at different times. "I just got the thrill of my lifetime," Luella says with a delighted smile, "because I saw the person who's in charge of the Big Sister office in Welland and she said that Lori (my first Little Sister) has just joined the Big Sister Organization and she has a Little Sister now."

Has being L.M. Montgomery's granddaughter affected your life in any way?

"Oh, no. How do you mean?"

People wanting to talk to you about her, asking you to make public appearances at various functions ...

"Oh, well, that's just been lately."

Can you relate a recent experience?

"Some young kids were putting on an *Anne of Green Gables* play in Welland. It sounded rather interesting, so I called to see if I could get a ticket. Before the thing started, it was announced that L.M. Montgomery's granddaughter was in

Luella Macdonald Veijalainen and Alexandra Heilbron enjoying tea at the Norval manse where L.M. Montgomery lived from 1926 to 1934.

Courtesy Kathy Gastle.

the audience. There were some people there who knew who I was, but they don't make a big deal of it. Well, after the announcement, good heavens. And of course, I had to stand up.

"Intermission time, I was surrounded by kids and finally I had to say, *Listen, I've got to go and get a drink of water.* They wanted my autograph, and I thought, 'I didn't do anything.' But they wanted me to sign their programs and stuff like that. Sometimes people go and buy one of my grandmother's books and want me to sign it, and I say, *But I didn't write this — this isn't my book.* Oh well, reflected glory and all that. I said to Karem, *You've got to read more of her books* [because fans of L.M. Montgomery will come up to you and want to discuss them with you. Karem is a Stephen King kind of a reader."

Have you seen *Road to Avonlea* or *Anne of Green Gables* on television?

"I like the *Anne of Green Gables* series. *Road to Avonlea*, I enjoy it as a series, it's fun. But not as an L.M. Montgomery kind of thing. The language they used is not the language that was spoken back then. The things they were talking about, tempers or emotions, they didn't use those terms. They might say, *Control your temper* or something like that, but they didn't talk about stuff the way they did on the show. Language is different now than it was back then. I guess they were doing it for today's audience."

Luella didn't enjoy the latest Anne film, *Anne of Green Gables: The Continuing Story*. "It just didn't seem right. The only thing in it that had anything to do with Anne was the title. People who watched it will think that's what the books were about.

"I met Jon Crombie, who played Gilbert, when I was at a restaurant in Toronto with my Little Sister several years ago. I couldn't resist — I said, *Look, there's Gilbert.* He ended up staying for ages. We were talking for so long that he was squatting at table level, he was so interested. We had a very pleasant chat."

In 1994 Luella heard that *The Wooden Hill*, a new stage play based on her grandmother's life, was being presented at the St. Lawrence Centre in Toronto. She called up for tickets and found that the final performance was that very night. "I thought, 'I've got to see this thing,'" Luella remembers. "I burnt the pavement driving into Toronto — I must have broken every speed limit!" There was a long lineup to get in to see the play, but Luella obtained her ticket and found her seat. While watching, she grew angrier and angrier at what was happening on stage, and during the intermission she spoke to an usher, explaining who she was, and asked to meet the cast afterwards. After the show, he led her to the dressing room where Rita Howell, the actress who portrayed L.M. Montgomery, was taking off her makeup.

"I chewed her out as if she were my grandmother," Luella recalls with a laugh. "I said, *You didn't like my father, did you!* And I burst into tears and she hugged me. She [Rita Howell] said it was probably the biggest compliment she'd gotten on her portrayal of my grandmother [that I'd related to her as if she actually were my grandmother]." It wasn't that the actress physically resembled L.M. Montgomery or even that she acted the way Luella remembers her grandmother acting, but her performance brought back the feelings she'd had while reading the published letters that L.M. Montgomery had written to her pen-pal G.B. MacMillan. "It was all Stuart this and Stuart that and Stuart and his gymnastics. Well, she had another kid, too."

"My grandmother probably should never have gotten married or had kids. She should have just kept to writing." Luella's oldest two children were boys, and they were different from each other, much in the same way Chester and Stuart were different. Lauri, the first born, was more distant and independent, while John Erik, the younger boy, was more affectionate. "It's easy to reach out to the one who comes close and wants to be cuddled," Luella explains, but she believes that perhaps the one who doesn't reach out is possibly even more in need of warmth and closeness than the other children.

When your grandmother died, you were almost eight years old. Did you go to the funeral?

"Oh, no. I just read about it in the newspaper. I remember getting weepy and crying, because I loved her and the news came as a shock."

In March 2000, Luella was invited by the Government of Prince Edward Island to travel to Japan to meet Japanese fans of *Anne of Green Gables*, a trip sponsored and promoted by the L.M. Montgomery Land Trust. "Aoi Nozawa [a writer with PEI Promotions, the LMM Land Trust in Japan, and the Lupins Anne of Green Gables Fan Club in Japan] was largely responsible for the event and for coaxing the Government of Prince Edward Island to support my going there. I have nothing but praise for their kind welcome to me — both from the fans and the people generally in Osaka," Luella says.

The event was called "The World of Anne of Green Gables: Commemorating the 125th Anniversary of the Birth of L.M. Montgomery," and was held on March 31, 2000. Luella was the special guest, and speakers included Aoi Nozawa and Yasuka Terashita (secretary of the Canadian Consul General of Japan). Luella was presented with Japanese versions of the Emily and Anne books, but what amazed and touched her most was how excited and thrilled the Japanese fans were to meet her — L.M. Montgomery's granddaughter — face to face.

Chapter Two
Mrs. Macdonald as an Employer

Because of her busy schedule, Maud found it necessary to hire a maid or house-keeper to help with the household chores. In the early years, Maud would write out lists of what she wanted her maids to do on a daily basis. She would often work side by side with her maids: Maud liked to cook and bake and would do much of that herself. Later on, she preferred to leave these tasks to the maids and would spend most of her days reading.

Maud frequently found fault with her helpers. They were usually young women who had to be trained to do things the way she liked having them done. She expected them to be cheerful at all times. They had to bake, clean, dust, do laundry, and prepare meals. When the Macdonald boys were small, the maids had to keep an eye on them. In addition, the maids were expected to live with the Macdonalds.

Here are first-hand accounts of Mrs. Macdonald from several of the people who worked for her.

L.M. Montgomery,
circa 1918.

Courtesy Prince Edward Island Public Archives and Records Office

Elsie (Bushby) Davidson

Born the daughter of an Ontario farmer on February 7, 1904, Elsie Bushby moved with her family to Leaskdale, Ontario, in 1917, when she was thirteen years old. The Bushbys joined the Presbyterian congregation where Reverend Ewan Macdonald was minister. In 1921 Maud asked seventeen-year-old Elsie to fill in for a week when Maud's current maid, Lily Meyers, was sick with tonsillitis. Maud liked cheerful Elsie's ready-to-learn attitude and hard work so much that she asked her to fill in on several further occasions when Lily went on vacations. Finally, when Lily quit the position in February 1925, Maud asked Elsie to work full time. Elsie's room in the Leaskdale manse was at the top of the stairs to the right. There was a door from Elsie's room that led directly to the trunk (storage) room, and from that room there were stairs that led downstairs to the kitchen area. The Macdonalds had the master bedroom to the left of the stairs, and the boys slept in the room across from the trunk room, at the front of the house.

How did you get the job?

"Well, I was a farmer's daughter and Mrs. Macdonald wanted help. I filled in when her maids were away on occasion, and when the last one left, Lil Meyers, Mrs. Macdonald asked me if I would be her maid and I was delighted. Mother was quite delighted as well to let me go because it was a nice start for me. And it was nice and handy to be going home only a mile and a quarter. Stuart and I used to walk down after dinner at night to my mother and father's and then we'd walk back home before dark."

Lily Reid (an early maid of Maud's), Chester, and Zella Cook, a Leaskdale neighbour.

Courtesy Isabelle St. John.

Did you live at the manse?

"Yes. Day and night. And I had all my Sundays off, but I just took every other Sunday, that is, to be free entirely. Mrs. Macdonald was very nice to work for. She had her work all planned and everything was nice."

Was there a lot of work?

"Just ordinary. We weren't slaves. She wrote out my work on a little pad and I had that to go by. As long as I done my work each day, I had time off to do as I liked. I often used to get the washing and the ironing done on Mondays, and then Tuesdays I just mended the clothes and looked after that part of it. That is, the socks. And then Wednesdays I'd just job around, but I used to have all the jobs done usually and then I had Wednesday to play."

What were you paid?

"I got twenty-two dollars a month. That's what I got for wages."

Was that quite a bit?

"Well, it wasn't bad. It wasn't bad at that time. And I had all my time free."

What did you do in your spare time?

"Oh, I used to go down to my mother's and see her, and I always was back for dinner at night. Or just knocked about if there wasn't anything, but there was always an odd chore you could do, and then Thursday I cleaned up the upstairs and Friday the living room and the library. Saturday, I worked in the kitchen."

What kind of lighting did they have? Was it electric?

"No. We used kerosene lamps and gasoline lamps. Mrs. Macdonald used to sit after supper, writing her book or her scraps [Maud had scrapbooks, both of her keepsakes and of her published stories and poems] or her diary."

Was there an indoor washroom?

"No. We went out in a hurry and came back in a bigger one [laughs]."

How was the house heated?

"With coal. Furnace. And there was a wood stove in the kitchen."

Did L.M. Montgomery like to bake?

"Yes. And she always made her own Christmas cake. She made her own wine, as well. She had some good wine, too. Dandelion, rhubarb, grape."

What other things did she bake?

"Mrs. Macdonald always done the first baking of any new recipe. If she was getting a new recipe, she tried it out first herself. And then if it suited her, why, I could go ahead and do it. And she always made the New Year's dinner and the Christmas dinner — the fowl — and she had ham for New Year's. And when Mrs. Macdonald done her ham, she'd mix up flour and water and roll it out, and

Elsie Bushby
Davidson.

she'd put this ham in the middle and fold that part over. And she'd bake it and it would take a whole day to bake. And when she took it out of that, she had to have the axe to break the crust. But oh boy, was that good. Had all the essences of the whole ham. Gee, it was good. Mrs. Macdonald was a very good cook. She was plain, but she was good."

I understand L.M. Montgomery liked to do handiwork as well.

"Oh, she was a great knitter, her hands were always busy."

When and where did she do her writing?

"She wrote in the morning, from nine till twelve in her living room. And then in the afternoon she'd be going back and forth through the house from the kitchen here through to the living room and into the library, whispering or talking out loud to herself. You wouldn't know what she was saying. And then at night she'd write these little remarks down or maybe she'd write them down when she'd think of it. Her notebook was kept on her desk. She'd go through that when she'd be going to write her book. She sort of took the best out of this and put it into that. Well, then she'd rewrite that again. It takes about a year to do a book. And then when she got through it, Mrs. Macdonald would send the manuscript off to have it typed. When it came back, it came back in long strips. Proofreading, she called it. I read all those books. Mrs. Macdonald would let me read the proofreading. And then she'd send it away again, and when it came back she'd have to read that book over again, to see if it was alright. Oh, there was a lot of work involved in it. She was a good author. And she was a good mother, too. Only, one thing. If the boys didn't like what they had to eat, they had to eat it whether they wanted it or not. She had a chair rung that she rapped them over the fingers with. And boy, that smacked. And they had to eat their porridge or whatever it was they didn't like. And I always said in my mind if I ever was a mother I wouldn't make my kids eat things that they didn't like and I never did, either."

Elsie remembers Stuart, Maud's youngest son, fondly. "I liked him awful well." He would often beg to accompany the girl when she went home to visit her mother. As for Chester, the older boy, Elsie says, "He was like his dad." She recalled that he was a great reader and would grab a handful of cookies right after breakfast before returning to bed to continue reading. After a short time, he would reappear for more cookies. This continued until, in desperation, Elsie hid the cookies in the cellar to save some for the rest of the family, knowing Chester wouldn't bother going down there for them. "He was as lazy as a pet coon," Elsie recalls with a laugh.

Did Mrs. Macdonald have to discipline the boys any other time, besides when they didn't eat their food?

"Not that I ever noticed. They were pretty good boys, you know. I don't know how she disciplined them at all. And I never knew that Mr. Macdonald was sick with a melancholy disease. I knew he was sick, but I had no idea what it was, exactly. He always just said he was going away for a holiday or something. He was tired, and he wanted a rest."

What sort of church work did Mrs. Macdonald do?

"Gee Winnigers, she'd come out and they got a Young People's [group] started there between the two of them. She was good at training the young people."

How would you describe Mr. Macdonald?

"He was very quiet. And he could be jovial, you know, when he was feeling very well. But this was what always got me. Oh, gosh, it used to make me so mad. I got mad, too. If I didn't have the dinner just on the table when he'd come and sit down at it, he'd go [taps her spoon on a glass], *Dinner in the dining hall! Dinner in the dining hall!* I could have shot the old beggar right down the drain. I can hear that cup rattle yet."

Was he joking?

"Oh, sure he was. Just, he thought he'd get my goat. Other times he used to kind of tease me a bit. But he wasn't so bad most of the time; he was always very good. I couldn't have anything bad to say about him; I didn't have many dealings with him."

While the Macdonalds were living in Leaskdale, they bought their first car. "Mr. Mac would drive in, saying, *Whoa, Sally!* or whatever he called it. He wasn't a good car driver. That's one thing. But he got along."

Did they have a horse as well?

"They had, before they got the car, and they had a horse when they went to Norval, too."

If Mrs. Macdonald wanted to go to Uxbridge, would she get the horse ready herself?

"No, no, no. He always got it ready."

Did the Macdonald family have any pets while you were with them?

"Dixie was the dog. Paddy was the cat. And Lucky [another cat], he had a history. Lucky came from Prince Edward Island. He was a grey cat, light grey with dark markings, and on the outside his fur had a design like a heart on the sides. He was really pretty. The other cat, Paddy, the Macdonalds liked him too, but they didn't like him as well as the one that came from Prince Edward Island. One day, Lucky went missing. And it was like a funeral around there. They all felt bad. He was such a nice cat. And I was outside one day, I don't know what I was doing, but I heard this meowing. So I went where I could hear it and it was coming from a barn. And I got him out and brought him home. I walked into the house and Mrs. Macdonald was in there and I said, *See what I found.* It was just like finding a new, lost friend. We all went haywire. Oh, were we ever tickled to see that cat. I tell you, he never went missing after that."

When Reverend Ewan Macdonald was given a new position as the minister in Norval, Ontario, which meant a move from Leaskdale, Maud was worried that young Elsie would become homesick if she came along. Elsie, however, was extremely excited about making the move and convinced Maud to let her keep her position.

"I went up to Norval with them, and there was a couple of old maids up there and they usually got their washing out ahead of anybody else. I said to Mrs. Macdonald, *They're not getting ahead of me!* So I got everything all ready Sunday night before I went to bed, and I got up at half past three Monday morning and was putting the socks on the line when they put their pillowcases out. That set them back. We got a big laugh over that. Oh boy, I was tickled when I beat those old MacPherson ladies."

What kind of a washing machine did you have?

"Oh, we had a real dilly. Oh, she was a dandy. There was a rubber, like a rock-er affair, it went back and forth and that's what you washed with."

Automatically?

"Oh, gosh, no! You done everything by hand. And you had to carry the water in and heat it, and then carry it out and empty it."

What time did your workday start?

"Well, we got up, we had breakfast at eight. Lunch at one and supper at six. When the boys would go to school and come home, we'd have lunch when they got home, maybe twelve or half past twelve. But ordinarily on Saturdays and Sundays we'd have it at about one o'clock."

How did you decide to leave Norval?

"Mrs. Macdonald didn't use me very nice at the tail end. She had a wicked lit-tle temper. She's not here to hear me, but she did."

What do you mean, she didn't "use you very nice"?

"She didn't like Rob Anderson, this guy that I was walking around with."

Despite Mrs. Macdonald's objections, Elsie was determined to go out with Rob, even though his parents didn't approve of the match either. Although he was a Norval boy, Rob was living in Toronto at that time, and the couple decided it would be easier for them to see each other if Elsie moved to Toronto as well and got a job there. Elsie told Mrs. Macdonald that her mother needed her at home in Leaskdale and gave her a month's notice. One night, long after every-one was in bed, Elsie and Rob found Mrs. Macdonald's diary in her desk and read some excerpts she had written about Elsie, including the fact that she knew Elsie had lied about her reason for leaving. Mrs. Macdonald must have known that they'd invaded her privacy, because the next day she paid Elsie her wages and told her she could leave immediately rather than finish off the rest of the month. "I never told any of this to anybody else, but I thought I was a lady by giving in my resignation when I did. And I offered to help train another girl if she needed. And it wasn't very nice [of her to dismiss me so abruptly]. But she was always good to me, only at the last she was just mad."

Elsie went home to Leaskdale, and she and Rob broke up soon after. "I was home pretty much the whole year and then I got work at the telephone office and stayed there for about ten years. Then I married and went out to my husband's farm in Sandford for about twenty-five years. And then I came into town [Uxbridge] and I got working at the hospital for six and a half years."

Elsie Davidson worked as a telephone operator in the early days of telephones in Ontario, for a company called Home Telephone. Towards the end of her time there, the company was purchased by Bell Telephone. In 1995 Bell Telephone honoured Mrs. Davidson as one of their "Telephone Pioneers of America" and sent her a certificate to show their appreciation for her hard work.

Did you ever see Mrs. Macdonald after you left Norval?

"No. They had an opening [unveiling ceremony] here in Uxbridge at the Town Hall with Mrs. Macdonald's picture. It's up at the Uxbridge-Scott Museum now. And Stuart was down here for the ceremony. I went around and I spoke to him and he didn't know me. I said, *Well I used to mend your socks for you and look after you.* And he said, *Elsie! My God, am I ever glad to see you.* Stuart was still this little darling that he was when I worked there. Oh, he was a cute kid."

Elsie has read the journals, and although it hasn't changed her feelings about Mrs. Macdonald, she realizes that a lot of people have changed their mind about the woman they respected as their minister's wife and as a famous author. "Mrs. Macdonald has put some dirty little things in several of her books and some I wish they hadn't been put in. It's caused a lot of hard feelings. Now Leaskdale hasn't the same respect for her that they used to have. There was things put in that book that were far better not said.

"Mary Rubio [co-editor of L.M. Montgomery's published journals] said that from her readings [of Montgomery's journals], she took it that Mrs. Macdonald thought of me as a daughter. I'll tell you one thing. She always prided herself in a nice pair of gloves and a nice hat. And her gloves — it hits me even yet — I make sure my gloves fit me nice. I learned a lot up there, in my upcoming. I was just at the age where I could be trained and I was one that would like to copy people. I have to be honest about it and be outright. It has made me the person that I am. Well, I don't know whether I've made a good job of it or not, but I feel that Mrs. Macdonald really put the good in me, if there's any there."

Helen (Mason) Schafer

*Helen Mason's mother was the Macdonalds' housekeeper in Norval from 1927 to
1931, and Helen and her mother lived at the manse with the Macdonald family.*

It was rare for Maud to have written absolutely no complaints about a maid in
her journals, but this seems to have been exactly the case with Helen's mother, Mrs. Mason. Perhaps it was because she was an avid reader, just as Maud was,
that the two women found a common ground and much to discuss. "Mother
read everything she could get her hands on. She read all the time. Anything
you wanted to know, Mother knew. She knew everything. She had a lot of
books," Helen remembers.

Helen Schafer.

Your mother and Mrs. Macdonald got along well.

"Very well. My mother was a good housekeeper and a good cook. I don't know how she ever did what she did and looked after me too. I must have been a very good child, sitting still in a corner. You know what a two-year-old can get into. I often wondered how mother ever did it. She made the meals, she did all bedding."

What was the manse like? Which was your room?

"At the front upstairs was our bedroom. It's an old-time house and I remember when mother shut the bedroom door there was a window up at the top of the door that you could open. Mother would put me to sleep and I remember looking up, and I don't know what they were standing on but both of them [Mrs. Mason and L.M.M.] were looking in and I was just lying there, looking around. They wanted me to sleep; they were having a garden party at night in the yard and I guess I was supposed to be sleeping."

How old were you then?

"Oh, maybe three. Mother remarried when I was six and we moved to Kitchener. Mrs. Macdonald said, *Your little girl gave you the job. I always wanted a little girl.* It worked out very well because I was very well behaved. No nonsense with me [laughs]. Mrs. Macdonald really enjoyed having me around. She gave me her old hats and dresses and beads and high heels and I'd go strut down the sidewalk in front of the manse and parade with a big purse and hat. But I could only go so far and then I had to come back again. I couldn't go anymore if I disobeyed.

"I remember the kitchen very well because my mother and Mrs. Macdonald would set me in a corner when they were both baking together in the big, old-fashioned kitchen. Mrs. Macdonald had three cats and Lucky was her favourite. She trained him to bring in anything that he'd catch. One day he came in through the screen door and dropped a snake on the kitchen floor right at Mrs. Macdonald's feet. They screamed and they jumped up on the table and stepped in the dough, they were so terrified. And Reverend Macdonald came in; he wondered what all the commotion was about.

"There was a back stairs; you went up the stairs and there was an old-fashioned bathroom. We always ate with the family in the dining room, but I don't remember that room as well as I remember the kitchen. I remember the back stairs because I think we went up the back stairs mostly in that house. I think everyone did, pretty well. I don't remember the living room very well either. Maybe we were never in it. Years ago, people didn't use the living room too much.

"Once, that same cat brought in a dead rabbit, took it up to Mrs. Macdonald's bedroom, and put it under the bed. Mother was told she could make the bed during the week but Friday was the cleaning day and she couldn't clean any other day but Friday. So Mother said to her, *There's quite a funny smell in your room. I'd like to see what it is, may I?* And Mrs. Macdonald said, *Oh, yes.* My mother looked under the bed and found the dead rabbit. Mrs. Macdonald no doubt wasn't around right at the time when Lucky brought it in.

"The big porch on the side of the house where the kitchen was, there was a cement plank and she had three dishes out there for the cats. Their names were Lucky, Pat, and Brownie. Brownie was an old stray cat. Lucky always would run to meet Mrs. Macdonald. No matter where she was, if she went down the street to shop, Lucky would run to meet her and come home with her, just like a dog. I remember Mrs. Macdonald telling Mother, *If you ever get a cat for Helen, always feed him liver once a week. They won't chase birds if you give them liver.*

"I never really got to know the boys. They were away at school. I knew who Stuart was and Chester, but they never played with me.

"I remember the night the mill burned. I was very nervous. Mother took me down there in her arms. I remember the flames. It kind of haunts me today yet, but it was quite exciting. People came from all over."

Did your mother speak about Mrs. Macdonald after you'd moved away?

"All the time. She remembered her as being just a kind, lovely lady. She never spoke of Mr. Macdonald much though. Well, he was a quiet man. He was a minister; he would go into his study and work there. I don't remember too much about him.

"I still like going back to Norval, driving past. I like reminiscing. Mrs. Macdonald went to Toronto to live shortly after we moved away. One time she was coming from Toronto to visit Mother in Kitchener and Mother had everything prepared. I was so disappointed when I came home from school and I didn't see her. I said, *Where is Mrs. Macdonald?* Mother said, *She phoned me and said she broke her arm and couldn't come.* She never did come to visit. They talked over the phone and sent letters, but she never came and I was so disappointed because I'd been looking forward to seeing her again."

Ethel (Dennis) Currie

Housekeeper to the Macdonald family in Norval, Ethel Dennis moved with them to Riverside Drive in Toronto.

In August 1934, when L.M. Montgomery stopped in at Norval's butcher shop to do some grocery shopping, she mentioned to proprietor Laura Robinson, who co-owned the store with her husband, that she needed a new housekeeper. Laura suggested her younger sister Ethel for the position. Twenty-year-old Ethel lived in a nearby town and just happened to be in Norval visiting Laura.

At the time Ethel was hired, Ewan Macdonald was nearing the end of a three-month stay in the Homewood Sanatorium in Guelph, Ontario. "He'd had a nervous breakdown and he came home about three weeks after I started the job," Ethel remembers. "Mrs. Macdonald had to get him what they called 'blue pills' at the drugstore in Georgetown. The doctor had ordered

Ethel Dennis at the time she worked for L.M. Montgomery.

Courtesy Gail and Bill Currie.

them. After she brought him the prescription from the drugstore, Mr. Macdonald took some of the pills and then Mrs. Macdonald went out to the store. In the meantime, the drugstore called and they wanted her, but she wasn't there.

"So they explained that there had been a mistake, that Mrs. Macdonald had been given the wrong kind of blue pills, and they were poisonous. They said to mix up an egg with soda and give it to Mr. Macdonald right away and I did. I told him the doctor had ordered it; I didn't know what else to tell him. I called the store and told Mrs. Macdonald to come right back. By the time she arrived, the doctor was there to give him some medicine. The pharmacist had called him and told him to come over right away. I was told later that if I hadn't had Mr. Macdonald drink that mixture right away, he could have died. The pharmacist who made the mistake lost his job over it."

Ethel was in attendance on October 4, 1934, when Maud's cousin, Marion Webb of Green Gables, was married by Reverend Macdonald in Norval. Ethel remembers the day quite clearly as a big event in the Macdonald household. "Marion got married to Murray Laird. Mrs. Macdonald had a supper for her and Murray and some of Murray's people. They were married in the manse. They were supposed to go out to Prince Edward Island to be married, but for some reason Murray couldn't go, so they had to cancel it and Marion came here instead."

Did you live with the family?

"Oh yes, I lived in with them."

Did Mrs. Macdonald have a list of jobs that she expected you to do?

"No, she would come down in the morning and tell me what she wanted for meals and work, and then, [at] house-cleaning time, instead of doing it once a year or twice a year, we'd do one room a month and she would always help me with it."

Did she help with any of the other housework?

"Not really. Just on my weekend off."

How often did you get a weekend off?

"Every other weekend."

Did Mrs. Macdonald have a recipe book?

"Oh, yes. She usually knew what she wanted."

Do you remember any of the recipes?

"No, there were too many of them. She had a lot of different dishes, supper dishes. And recipes for pickles."

Do any events that occurred in Norval stick in your mind?

"One time Mrs. Macdonald invited the Barracloughs for supper. They used to run the knitting mill at Glen Williams. And she clean forgot about it until they were at the door. [Laughs.] At the door for supper — and she hadn't told me. She just forgot and that was it. We scurried around and got something together for supper anyway, but we were pretty shocked."

As the minister's wife, Maud had church meetings to attend or preside over. Ethel remembers that these were always held in the church rather than at home, as the church was located right next to the manse. "She'd just step out of the house and went across the lawn to the church."

It was a big day for both the Macdonalds and Ethel when the Macdonalds moved to their new home, "Journey's End," on Riverside Drive in Toronto in 1935. There was quite a commotion in the neighborhood. "They knew it was her moving in. There were a lot of young ones, and of course, they were all hollering and yelling, 'Lucy Maud Montgomery!'"

Did children come to the door to see her?

"I think they did later on, not just right then. She went out on speaking engagements often."

Was she different in public than she was at home?

"No, she was just herself."

Was Riverside Drive a very wealthy neighbourhood?

"Oh, yes. They were just building whole new houses."

What was the house like?

"It was a three-storey home. It was quite nice."

Was it very luxurious?

"Yes. And no. She wasn't the type to want everything like they do now."

How would you describe Mrs. Macdonald?

"She was quiet, she was real friendly, but there was no silly stuff about her."

How did she dress? Like everyone else, or more elegantly?

"No, she just dressed like anybody else. She was particular about herself, but she didn't try and overdress or anything."

How was she getting along with her husband?

"Good. He was getting a bit forgetful and had trouble sleeping at night. She had her ups and downs with him."

Did she have a particular time of day that she would devote to her writing?

"Oh, no. She'd be up in her bedroom all the time. That's where she would write, mostly."

Did she have a desk there?

"Yes."

Was she an early riser? What time did she get up in the morning?

"Yes. Well, not real early. I was the one to get up and get breakfast. I couldn't tell you right off. Around eight o'clock or something like that."

Ethel Dennis Currie today.

Did she have any hobbies?

"No, I don't think so. She was too busy writing."

Needlepoint, sewing?

"No, just mending."

What were meal times like?

"Well, she'd be sitting at one end of the table, and Mr. Macdonald would be at the other, and she would have a book on one side [of her plate] reading it and then on the other side she'd have a scribbler and pencil and she'd take something she wanted out of the one book and write it in the other one."

At the dinner table?

"Mm-hm. Anytime. And Mr. Macdonald, he'd be at the other end, reading."

And the boys?

"Yes, everyone."

Everyone was reading at the dinner table?

"Oh, maybe once in a while not, but usually. They were a quiet family."

Did the family have any pets?

"No, just the two cats. They were really hers, I think. The two cats were both gone by the time I left to be married. Mrs. Macdonald had a ravine at the back [of her house on Riverside] and a rock garden. She had two rocks from Prince Edward Island that she used to sit on when she was reading or doing writing work. She'd had them shipped up by freight to Toronto and put one on each cat's grave. The man who delivered them from the train didn't know what it was all about. He said, *Good God, couldn't you folks find enough stones in Ontario?* [Laughs.] Mrs. Macdonald was in the room right above the front door when he said that. I don't know yet whether she heard it or not. It was so comical, you know."

In 1935 L.M. Montgomery wrote of having a problem with sciatica and neurasthenia. Was she ill at that time?

"She had that problem of shaking her head and her hands would shake, but that's all I can remember."

Do you remember any of her friends from Prince Edward Island coming to visit?

"Oh, yes. They'd come once in a while. They called her Aunt Maud."

Did she talk about growing up in Prince Edward Island?

"Not about growing up there, but she thought more of that than anyplace."

Did she often go there on vacation when you worked for her?

"Oh, every year she went, for two or three weeks."

What colour was her hair?

"Dark brown."

What was her voice like?

"She didn't have a strong voice. It was quiet, she never hollered at you or any-thing."

Would you say that working for Mrs. Macdonald was a pleasant experience?

"Oh, yes. She wasn't interfering in any way with me or anybody else. She couldn't have been any better. It was just like being at home."

What was the atmosphere like in the house? Was it a pleasant one?

"Oh, yes. It was quiet. They all read. At least, she did, so the boys did too. They all read a lot."

How old were the boys while you were there?

"Gosh, they were going to university, so they must have been as old as I was. Chester, he was going through for a lawyer and Stuart was a medical student."

Did the boys get along?

"Yes, but I wouldn't say they were real close. They never talked that much to each other."

Was she usually happy?

"Yes, oh, yes. She had a lot on her mind. Writing books and then there was a little bit of trouble with the one boy, Chester. You know what I mean, he was a worry, but Stuart, he was good."

What sort of trouble did she have?

"Well, Chester got married and his mother didn't know anything about it, and when they had the first child, she didn't know about it until after they moved from Norval. Luella, his wife, lived at her family's home in Norval while Chester was going to university in Toronto. He would stay at the house on Riverside during the week and go to Luella's place on the weekends. So he could tell his mother anything and she'd believe it. Well, I guess she found out everything in time."

How upset was Mrs. Macdonald when she found out about the marriage?

"Oh, she was quite upset. It was a lot of money, too, putting him through university, and then she had the expense of supporting them as well."

She was supporting the couple?

"Yes, she was then. And they had another child later; that made it two to look after."

Was she happy to have grandchildren?

"Oh, yes. Luella would come to visit with them once in a while. Mrs. Macdonald was good to them, gave them lots — you know what I mean. But when the second child was born, she didn't know a thing about it. It was my weekend off. I was upstairs getting ready to go. I wasn't married yet, but my fiancé, Gordon, would come and pick me up. I heard the phone ring and she was talking to somebody, but I didn't know what it was, so we went out to go home and Gordon asked me, *What's the matter with Mrs. Macdonald?* I said, *I don't know. Well*, he said, *She's out there walking up and down the road*. She was wringing her hands and she looked upset. And then Stuart went out and talked to her and got her to come back in the house. You see, she'd just gotten the phone call that there was another baby and she hadn't known a thing about it. Luella hadn't been over that much lately. Mrs. Macdonald had to foot the bill and everything. She was upset about that. She didn't have it easy.

"Chester lied to her so much. And how stupid Chester was. Well, he was. We'd be cleaning upstairs. The third floor was for the maid, but instead of that I slept down on the second floor and the boys were up on the top. So anyway, we were up this day cleaning their room and Chester had a diary and left it sitting on top of the desk. That's how stupid he was, left it out in the open. Mrs. Macdonald picked it up and there it was, and she read it. Well, he was going out with women [while he was married] and I knew it. One time he told his mother he was going somewhere, he made up a lie about where he was, but he wasn't where he said, and she read that in the book. And Luella, she came down one weekend to visit and took the little girl upstairs; it was time to go to bed and she went to bed and was reading a book. He was downstairs — he came down and got the phone and took it to where no one could hear what he was saying. I knew what he was doing, alright. Calling his friend [instead of spending time with his wife and child]."

On March 21, 1937, Ethel Dennis and Gordon Currie were married at the Macdonalds' home on Riverside Drive, with Reverend Macdonald performing the ceremony. Before the wedding, Ethel's friend and matron of honour held a cup and saucer shower at the house on Riverside. Maud presented Ethel with a cup and saucer at the shower, and she attended the wedding. Her wedding gift to the couple was a silver tray embossed with a pattern of grapes. The Curries have four boys (Don, David, Bill, and Jim), five grandchildren, and three great-grandchildren.

Ethel (Swindlehurst) Webb

It is interesting that while Maud often complained in her journals about her husband's mental difficulties, in January 1940, when Ethel Swindlehurst worked for her, she was able to hide Ewan's illness and her own despair from those who knew her, even from someone living and working in her home. Maud herself was only a couple of years away from her death.

When Anita Webb, one of L.M. Montgomery's later housekeepers, had to go to Prince Edward Island to help her brother Keith, whose wife had just died, she asked her friend Ethel to fill in for her on Riverside Drive for a month. Ethel, a recent graduate from a nursing course in Toronto, was a friend of all the Webb sisters, Marion, Anita, and Lorraine. She would eventually become Keith Webb's second wife.

In earlier years, such as when Elsie Bushby had worked for the Macdonalds, Maud had worked side by side with her maids, doing many of the chores herself and supervising the baking. By the time the Macdonalds moved to Toronto, however, Maud was content to let her maids do most of the work by them-

Ethel Swindlehurst
Webb.

selves. Now in her sixties, with her husband retired from the ministry, Maud must have finally allowed herself to slow down.

What kind of work were you asked to do for L.M. Montgomery?

"Just all the housework. I made her favourite cookies, Boston drop cookies."

Did she help with any of the baking?

"No."

Did she do any housework?

"Very little. She spent a lot of time reading. I don't remember whether the boys were there or not. Oh, they would be, I imagine. Chester married a girl near Georgetown here."

What was her relationship with her husband at that time?

"Oh, I think they got along alright."

How did you get the job?

"It was through Keith's sister, you see. She wanted somebody to take her place while she was in Prince Edward Island. I had worked for Marion a good many times, that's how I got to know the family. Keith was the last one I met. And the rest of the family had all visited when I was working there."

How old were you at the time?

"I was born in 1910, so I'd be twenty-five or something like that. Maybe more. Anita wanted a break, [to] go down to the Island for a month and help out Keith when his wife died."

Chapter Three
Maud as Neighbour and Friend

Maud was a most cordial neighbour by all accounts. She was distinguished. She always dressed nicely and carried herself properly. Maud had a warm side and proved to be someone who cared very much about other people. When children in the village were sick, she went to check on them to see how they were doing. She not only lent money to neighbours and friends, but also helped out when complete strangers asked her for loans during a difficult time. She always spared whatever she could to help someone in need.

Maud was well liked in all the communities she lived in. The people of Leaskdale put out a booklet honouring her memory after she passed away. They successfully campaigned to have the manse where she and her family had lived

This postcard, which the Macdonalds sent to their parishioners, shows (from left) Stuart, Ewan, Maud, and Chester. Underneath Maud wrote, "Greetings from the manse folks."

Courtesy Wilda and Harold Clark.

from 1911 to 1926 declared a historic site by the Province of Ontario in 1965, and in that year a large plaque was placed in the front lawn. In 1997 the federal government declared the manse a national historic site and another plaque was mounted on the house itself. Norval, where Maud and her family had lived from 1926 to 1935, has an annual event in honour of her memory on the weekend closest to her birthday (November 30). In that town there is also a Lucy Maud Montgomery Garden with a plaque in her honour, as well as a plaque honouring not only Maud, but also her husband Ewan, in the church where he served as minister.

Ewan is remembered in different ways by the different people who knew him. While some describe him as jovial and teasing, others remember him as gruff or dour. As Maud related in her journals, he suffered from religious melancholia, and perhaps the people who remember him as dour saw him when he was experiencing one of his attacks. Normally, he was quite friendly and sociable, although he tended to be a quiet man and was never as outgoing as Maud.

On Riverside Drive in Toronto, just a few steps away from the house where she lived her final years, there is a small park named the Lucy Maud Montgomery Parkette. A plaque mounted by the Toronto Historical Board tells about Maud's years as a resident of Toronto. This tribute clearly shows that Maud was well liked in her Toronto community and that her generosity and many kindnesses were much appreciated.

Maud sent this Christmas postcard to a neighbour in Leaskdale, signed from Chester.

Courtesy Isabelle St. John.

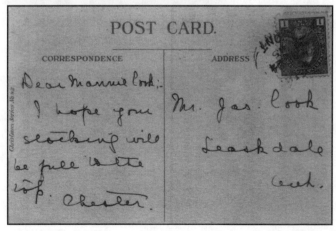

Ed Campbell Jr.

Ed's mother, Nora Lefurgey Campbell, was one of Maud's closest friends in Cavendish. When the Campbell family moved to Ontario, Ed looked forward to meeting the woman he'd heard his mother speak of so fondly.

L.M. Montgomery didn't have many close friends with whom she could share her love of nature and interest in intellectual matters, but when she did find such a kindred spirit, she deeply treasured the friendship. Nora Lefurgey was among that elite group of people.

A native of Prince Edward Island, Nora taught at the small, one-room Cavendish schoolhouse from September 1902 to June 1903. The school was located in the woods just across the road from the farm where Maud lived with her grandmother. The two young women, both highly intelligent and well educated, quickly became close friends. They waded in the surf of the Cavendish shore together, took long walks, shared their hopes and dreams, and laughed, something that was otherwise lacking in Maud's life. They took turns writing a "comic diary," which included humorous descriptions of their adventures, illustrated with cartoons that they drew themselves.

In July 1904 Nora returned to Cavendish for a holiday. The two women spent many carefree days together, revisiting old haunts and taking photographs of each other. Maud remembered that time long afterwards, and one of those days in particular she declared to be one of the few perfect days of her life.

Nora and Maud corresponded for years, but somehow they had lost contact. In 1928, while living in Norval, Maud received a letter from Nora to say that she and her husband, Edmund (Ned) Campbell, and their children were now living in Toronto. Naturally, Maud was thrilled that her friend was living only a short radial ride away, but her pleasure was mixed with doubt. She feared that perhaps they had both changed too much in the meantime for their friendship to have survived. Her fears were in vain; the two women fell on one another with joy the moment they saw each other. Ed remembers this reunion between his mother and her good friend, how they laughed and talked non-stop.

"I first saw Maud in 1928, when I was ten years old. She came and visited us in Toronto. I remember quite vividly seeing this, to my eye, very large woman, rather frightening actually because she was so commanding in personality. But it was something to see her and my mother acting like little girls; they were so happy to see each other and their conversation was so animated. I could see the both of them almost catch fire. They were just transcended with the delight of being back in one another's company again."

Ed Campbell Jr., ten years old, in Norval.

Courtesy Ed Campbell Jr.

Nora Lefurgey Campbell, Maud's kindred spirit.

Courtesy Ed Campbell Jr.

The two friends visited each other often, and on one occasion when Maud stayed overnight in Toronto, they took out their old "comic diaries" and laughed heartily at the intentional silliness of the entries they had written years earlier.

Ed accompanied his mother several times when she visited Maud in Norval. He remembers one particular visit: "Maud invited my mother, my brother, and me out to visit them and stay with them for a number of days in Norval. Her husband, the Reverend Macdonald, was the pastor out there in the Presbyterian church. It was in the summertime, probably 1929 or 1930, and I can remember it was such a stimulus to me, seeing my mother and Maud together once again. But I could sense that Maud's marriage to Macdonald was not a joyful thing. I won't say that they were fighting or anything, and they weren't speaking crossly one with the other, but I could sense that there was not much affection existing between the two of them."

During that same visit, the family sat down to dinner in the dining room of the Norval manse. Ed was only eleven or twelve at the time, and today he doesn't remember the particulars, but for some reason, at one point, Mr. Macdonald got up from the table and came back with a shotgun, which he pointed at Nora's head. "In what turned out to be playfulness, the reverend took a shotgun and threatened my mother. He was at the end of the table, she was sitting on his left hand, and I was sitting at the other end of the table. I knew enough about firearms to know that, even as a joke, it wasn't very funny. I'm sure it was meant as a joke, but it just startled me and certainly startled my mother at the time because she also lived a life where she was aware of the danger of firearms. It turned out that it was a fun thing in his mind and I can only deduce that there must have been some sort of related conversation going around the table with Maud and my mother and the reverend." After that incident Nora referred to her dear friend as "my poor Maud."

Stuart and Chester, both older than Ed, were at home during the Campbell family's visit. "I met Stuart and Chester Macdonald and knew them, but I didn't particularly like Chester, although I never had anything specific to complain about him. Stuart was a teenager at that time and had his teenage friends and didn't pay much attention to someone so much younger. But I liked him and I admired him. I can remember him as being a very fine looking and pleasant young man."

In 1940 Ed Campbell signed up with the Royal Canadian Artillery and was shipped overseas. He never saw Maud again, but he did have a chance meeting with Stuart, who had also enlisted. "Strangely enough, the next time I saw any of that family was in the brasserie in Picadilly Circus in London. I was sitting there drinking a beer and lo and behold, at a nearby table, there was Stuart Macdonald. He was in uniform in the Royal Canadian Navy and I think he was a doctor."

Ed's most vivid memories of L.M. Montgomery are of the warmth and joy he witnessed in the relationship she shared with his mother. "A prominent part of *Anne of Green Gables* is the close friendship that Anne had with Diana. I know that in its time that sort of thing was very usual. I don't know whether it still is. But that was the sort of relationship that existed between Maud and my mother. They cheered one another up."

Mary (Coupland) Maxwell

Born and raised on a farm in Norval, Ontario, Mary Maxwell has written a book called To Walk A Country Mile. *A history of Norval from the time it was founded, this book includes stories about the people (including Maud) who lived in the tiny village up to the present date. Mrs. Maxwell was a classmate of Maud's son Stuart, and she fondly shares her memories of the Macdonald family.*

When the Macdonalds arrived in Norval in 1926, Mary was twelve years old. An avid reader, Mary had several books by L.M. Montgomery. "I read my first Anne book when I was eight years old," Mary explains, "but she was just the lady who wrote the books. I didn't know that she was that famous. My mother seemed to think she was somebody special and my aunt was thrilled to pieces that she came, but as far as I was concerned, she was just Stuart's mother."

Mary was a classmate of Stuart Macdonald's. "I knew Stuart very well. We were in the same entrance class. Stuart was the pride and joy of our class. Everybody loved him. He was great fun — a very clever boy and very well liked among all the girls and boys. Stuart was very helpful, would help anyone out anytime. He was just a great kid."

In 1928 Stuart joined his older brother, Chester, at St. Andrew's, a private boarding school in Newmarket. "You didn't see much of him in the village after he went away to private school. But Mrs. Macdonald kept him behind an extra year before letting him go away to school. She had such pleasure out of Stuart that she didn't want to see him leave home."

Chester wasn't as well known in Norval because he spent the school year away in Newmarket. "I didn't see Chester very much. One summer he worked in the flour mill for a while, but I think his mother didn't approve of that kind of work for him."

As she had in Cavendish and Leaskdale, in addition to her writing duties, Maud managed to fit in plenty of work on behalf of the church. "Mrs. Macdonald was a tremendous help in the Norval and Union Presbyterian churches. She taught Bible class, coached the young people's plays, and took a leading part in the Norval Community Old-Tyme Concerts held in the parish hall. Those concerts were the highlight of the year because they were just so good."

What part did Mrs. Macdonald take in the concerts?

"She would recite and she coached the plays. As well, Young People's [church group] would put on plays under her direction and perform them all over the place. There was so much of that kind of activity because there were few radios and no television. In fact, a lot of people at that time still didn't have hydro.

"I remember those wonderful concerts very well. Geordie Gollop in a tall silk hat singing "Can She Make a Cherry Pie, Billy Boy?" and Garfield McClure singing "My Grandfather's Clock." Mrs. Macdonald also used to write skits for the programs. And for our school concerts, she would write something for Stuart to recite. It was always pretty funny. The one I remember best was when Stuart read a short recitation entitled 'And Stuart Gets the Neck,' which was also the

Mary Coupland Maxwell signing her book *To Walk a Country Mile.*

Courtesy Mary Coupland Maxwell.

last line of every verse. Apparently, when they had company at the manse and chicken was on the menu, Stuart came up short. I have often wondered if that bit of verse ever turned up among her papers."

Mary also remembers an event that was talked about for years afterwards. In the summer of 1926, L.M. Montgomery was asked to speak to a group of Girl Guides. They were holding a jamboree on the Credit Valley flats on land owned by the Upper Canada College of Toronto, and Maud agreed to entertain them at their final campfire evening. "Marion Noble picked her up at the manse in a horse and buggy, and when L.M. Montgomery stepped out of the door, she was dressed in the same beautiful outfit she had worn earlier to meet Prince George and the Prince of Wales. A lovely dress and hat, white gloves, the whole bit. She was absolutely delighted with the Credit Valley scenery. All the tents nestled against the wooded hills. She told them the story of the wreck of the *Marco Polo,* a shipwreck that occurred on the shores of Cavendish when she was a small girl, and the girls were thrilled. L.M. Montgomery said she was honoured to be asked to speak to those girls, and in her own way, she honoured the Guides by dressing as she had for royalty."

How did she dress on a daily basis?

"Beautifully, always. Very nicely dressed. I don't think you'd ever have seen her on the street untidily dressed. She was a charming, gracious woman, with a soft voice that matched her personality. There was no inkling in her manner of the stress she was living under at home. As we learned much later, her husband, the Reverend Ewan, suffered from a mental difficulty which made it difficult for her to communicate with him."

Do you remember her husband?

"Yes. He was not as outgoing as she was, but he was very highly thought of. People who knew him well said he was a good conversationalist. But many times he was more aloof than she was. I guess he held back; he was more reserved.

A postcard of Stuart Macdonald that Maud sent to friends.

Courtesy Isabelle St. John.

He was inclined to be a dour man, but under it all he had a wit and sense of humour that perhaps didn't always show. And probably he never did understand his wife's love of life — the joy she found in everyday things. Mrs. Macdonald was an all around capable woman; in her Norval years she wrote several books. How she juggled the time between her church duties, her work, and her unpredictable husband, we will never know. Mrs. Macdonald was always very sensitive to her environment. She loved beauty, loved the flowers in her garden and those of the village gardens, the pines on Russell's hill and her beloved cat. Such happy memories. I'm very glad to have known that gracious lady."

Norma Urquhardt

A resident of Leaskdale as a child, Norma lived in nearby Uxbridge at the time of this interview. Her home was a cozy one, with afghans decorating the furniture and handiwork in process visible. Miss Urquhardt took an avid interest in her community and was constantly busy. Even as she relaxed at home, she spent her time knitting and crocheting.

Norma's main connection to Maud Montgomery is through the Leaskdale church as well as the Leaskdale school. Born May 20, 1905, she was six years old when Maud arrived as a new bride in Leaskdale in 1911. Although Norma's family usually attended the Methodist church, located just down the road from the Presbyterian church where Montgomery's husband, Reverend Ewan Macdonald, was minister, Norma regularly attended meetings of the Young People's Group at the Presbyterian church.

"My family lived on the 6th Concession, which was a mile and a quarter west of Leaskdale, and my acquaintance at the church was mostly through the Young People's. That was a group of young people that met during the week," Norma recalls.

Who organized that group?

"Well, Mrs. Macdonald had quite a bit to do with it. She used to come often and have parts in it and everything like that."

What exactly was her role in the Young People's Group?

"Well, quite often she would speak on some subject that was of interest to young people."

Did she direct any of the plays?

"Oh, yes. That was her strong point."

Norma Urquhardt at her home in Uxbridge.

Were you in any of the plays she directed?

"I was in some of the Christmas concerts that she organized at the church. I can remember being there when we were practising an old-fashioned drill and we marched to the music. She was our instructor, and boy, she got cross at us because we didn't do it the way she wanted us to do it! [Laughs.] Of course, that was L.M. Montgomery. She was a perfectionist. And she wanted us to be perfectionists along with her. It didn't work out that way; all we were was a bunch of school kids!" [Laughs.]

Do you remember how Mrs. Macdonald was usually dressed?

"Well, I don't remember anything that stands out, but when she spoke in public, she'd have a lovely dress on with a nice lace collar and her hair up on her head, the way she always wore it. She was very dressy when she went out to do anything like that."

Were you aware that she was famous?

"Not at that time, no. As a kid, I didn't. If I'd have been older, I might have."

Have you read any of her books?

"Oh, I've read them all."

Did you read them then, or after?

"Both."

Do you remember Chester or Stuart Macdonald?

"Oh, I remember the boys, yes. I went to school up at Leaskdale and that's where the boys went to school."

What were they like?

"They were just boys, let's just put it that way. They were younger than me. In those days, you didn't have all the school nurses and all the rest of it that we have today. But we had a medical officer of health that came to the school every once in a while. One day Mrs. Macdonald and Dr. McClintoch, he was the medical officer of health for our area, came to the school. She was standing at the back with the teacher, and Dr. McClintoch was up at the front examining all the children. Of course, after he'd been there a little while, we realized what he was doing. He was examining us for head lice. So that was all very well; he went all over all of us. After he got through, he didn't come to the back to speak to Mrs. Macdonald privately, which he should have done. He stood up

Maud with Chester in
Leaskdale, circa 1913.

Courtesy Isabelle St. John.

at the front and said, *Mrs. Macdonald, you take your two boys home and clean them up. They're the only two in the school that have head lice.*

"Well, of course, she was simply like a balloon with a pin prick in it. She just popped. She was so mad, she just grabbed those boys and she went down that road — we had to walk about three-quarters of a mile — and she had a boy in each hand, and boy, she went down that road like a puppy with his tail between his legs. Poor Mrs. Macdonald. She was so embarrassed and so angry. You couldn't blame her. Kid and all as I was, I didn't blame her for being mad. I'd have been mad if it had been me, I know."

Why was she there for that particular examination?

"She had made the complaint that there was head lice in the school. Which was almost a disgrace in those days. But getting back to your question, we were all children together and we all played together, but I just can't pick out any special things about the boys. They were all right. We liked them at school. They were good kids."

What kind of things did all the children do together?

"We played games out in the yard. In the wintertime, we went sleigh riding and skating. There was a flat place out behind the school where the water always settled, and it would freeze over and we'd skate."

What kind of a school was it? How many rooms were there?

"Just one room. One teacher and one room. She had to teach all the grades at the same time."

How many children were in the school when you were a student?

"I'd say there'd be about twenty or maybe a few more. It varied from year to year."

In 1939, Norma Urquhardt became a teacher at the very one-room school in Leaskdale where she'd been a pupil not long before. She worked as a teacher for many years at various other schools in the district until her retirement.

Do you remember her husband?

"Oh, yes. Oh, he was very gruff. He was a handsome man. My parents and I didn't go to that church on a regular basis, but we had been there quite often, especially on special occasions. Nobody wanted the Macdonalds to leave [in 1926 when Reverend Macdonald was given a new post as minister at the Norval Presbyterian church]."

Did you hear about Mrs. Macdonald's death?

"Oh, yes. I visited both their graves when I went down to Prince Edward Island. And that's really the extent of my memories. It was quite a long time ago."

Joan (Browne) Carter

Born October 13, 1925, Joan was only a baby when the Macdonalds arrived in Norval. When they left in 1935, she was just nine, but because she lived right in town, Joan saw L.M. Montgomery frequently. The famous author left a vivid impression on the youngster.

Joan's family took part in Norval's famous Old-Tyme Concerts, which were held in the parish hall. She remembers some of the skits, including her mother and another Norval resident, Geordie Gollop, singing "Bicycle Built for Two" on a stationary two-seater. In fact, Joan and her brother are in a photograph taken of L.M. Montgomery and the other performers in one of the Old-Tyme Concerts.

"The one really clear memory I have of L.M. Montgomery, other than [of] her dressed up on stage, is that she would be walking to the post office to get the morning mail as I was going to school. And I have a very clear memory of saying, *Good morning Mrs. Macdonald,* and she was talking to herself. Her

L.M. Montgomery (far left) with the cast of an Old Tyme Concert in Norval, circa 1933. Joan is seated far right, facing the stage. Her brother is the boy at far left, facing the camera.

Courtesy Kathy Gastle.

mouth was moving. But she walked right past me and then said, *Good morning.* She'd be past you before she'd answer. Another young fellow in the village, Bill Pomeroy, who's five years younger than I am, he has the same memory of talking to her and she'd be past before she would reply. I got the feeling she was off in another world, a dream world."

Would that happen frequently?

"Quite often."

Did you know her sons?

"I knew Stuart. I only knew Chester vaguely because he was away at school. Stuart was in school here, and we were really impressed by him. He was a beautiful diver. Everybody swam every day in the Credit River. Stuart did a beauti-

Joan Browne Carter in Norval.

ful swan dive. Stuart later did gymnastics at university. He used to come to our house. One Christmas he and his girlfriend Joy came over to our house and decorated our Christmas tree."

How did L.M. Montgomery dress?

"I don't remember that, but a minister's wife usually dressed subdued. No bright colours. In fact, thinking back to those days, Presbyterians really dressed competitively for church. They went as if they were the elite class of the area. Maybe they were. They were mostly pretty successful farmers.

"I was only nine when she left and I wasn't Presbyterian, so I would have no occasion to go to the Presbyterian church, but we did go to the concerts. I don't remember being particularly impressed that she was famous, but I think she really did something for the village. She was famous to me as a child, because she was the Presbyterian minister's wife. The ministers and their wives were important people in the village."

Ethel (Bignell) Haines

Ethel Bignell was born in England in 1909, and her family came to Canada when she was eleven. From 1920 to 1929 she lived in Norval, where her parents owned and ran the Hollywood Hotel located at the town's main intersection. Ethel is a jolly woman with pleasant memories of dating Chester Macdonald.

"There was a Young People's Group that used to meet at the manse where they [the Macdonalds] lived. Mrs. Macdonald used to organize and direct different plays and I was in one of those. We used to go around to different places and put this play on. She was a very good director. I knew Mrs. Macdonald was a writer, but at the time I hadn't read any of her books. I've read many of them since. I've got one that was her journal, but I wasn't very fond of that," Ethel admits with a laugh. "I was really disappointed in that one."

Ethel wasn't mentioned in Maud's journals, but "my younger brother George is. He and Stuart evidently went skating and ended up in Huttonville and it was too late to come home and they walked home. They didn't get

Ethel Bignell Haines.

home until nine at night." Ethel was already married and living away from home at the time, so she didn't know anything about the incident until she read about it in Maud's journal. When asked if her brother was the "Sparky" in the journal, Ethel laughed at the memory of her small brother's nickname. "Yes. Sparky." However, she noted that Maud misspelled their family name throughout as "Bignall" instead of the correct spelling, "Bignell."

How did you meet Chester?

"He wasn't around the village that much because he was away at school. I do remember seeing him one time walking down the street and he looked so nice, you know. I don't know how we really got together, to tell you the truth. But I know we used to go to Georgetown on dates. The radial car was running then from Toronto to Georgetown and we would go to the show. He never had a car when I went out with him. I guess he wasn't old enough. I wouldn't have been any more than seventeen, I suppose."

What do you remember about Mrs. Macdonald?

"She was friendly. She was well thought of. But I didn't realize that her husband was ill until after I read it in her journal. I never heard anybody speak badly of him as a minister. I stayed at their house one night. The Macdonalds went to a play in Toronto with their housekeeper, Mrs. Mason. I knew Mrs. Mason quite well. We used to talk a lot, so they had me stay there and look after Mrs. Mason's little girl, Helen, while they all went to the play in Toronto."

Do you remember anything about how Mrs. Macdonald dressed?

"She always wore a big hat. Other than that, I couldn't tell you. I don't think I paid that much attention."

Dorothy (Watson) McLean

Dorothy Watson lived a few doors away from the Macdonald family in Norval. Born May 3, 1913, she remembers L.M. Montgomery very well.

"My clearest memory of L.M. Montgomery was her daily walk to Barnhill's store for the mail each morning. My father was a baker and we had a grocery store on Guelph Street. Where we lived, we were a short distance from the Presbyterian church and the manse, which was at the corner of Guelph and Draper. Several times during her nine years in Norval I happened to be outside our store, just a couple of feet from the sidewalk, when Mrs. Macdonald happened to be walking by for the mail. She never once looked my way or spoke to me. She was busy talking to herself. All the way down and back up the street, her lips were moving. She would turn her head from side to side and smile and nod. I thought that maybe she was composing a book or a story. I never spoke to her because I didn't want to interrupt this imaginary conversation she seemed to be enjoying. She was always beautifully dressed, wearing a pretty hat decorated with garnished flowers, feathers, or bows. She had a stately walk, which, along with her stylish dress, gave the impression of an important person.

"When the Macdonalds first came to Norval, their eldest son, Chester, attended a private boarding school. But Stuart was in the senior fourth grade at Norval School. That would be the equivalent of grade eight today. I was in that grade, too.

Dorothy Watson McLean.

Stuart was very clever. He was maybe a couple of years or so younger than most of us. He was well liked, outgoing, cheerful, and ready for fun. Stuart passed his entrance exams for high school that year; however, his mother thought that he was too young to leave home. She wanted him to attend the same private school that Chester attended. That would mean he would only be home on holidays and he was the last child to leave home. So she had Stuart repeat his grade. He was unhappy with this decision, as you can well imagine.

"Stuart enjoyed the swimming in summer [in the Credit River] and the skating and tobogganing in winter, and participated in all the village sports. He was a 'clip' — always full of mischief and ready for any kind of fun. My friend Mary Maxwell had long hair in braids down her back. She sat right in front of Stuart in class, and one day he put her pigtail into his inkwell. He only did it once because after that she made sure that her hair wasn't behind her! Oh, he was a clip. And very clever in school, too. He went on to become a doctor in Toronto.

"I had two brothers, one older [Mac] and one younger [Lee], and our house was the place where the kids would gather. The Macdonald boys would come over, too. I remember one time when I was about fifteen. Chester was chasing me around the dining room table while my mother and father were sitting out on the verandah! There was no way I was going to let him catch me! At last he had to give up, but he said, *I'll never be married until I have you for a wife*, because he was bound that I was going to marry him and if I didn't, he wouldn't get married at all. He was girl-crazy and so I didn't want anything to do with him. He married a girl from the country several years later.

"I enjoyed the Old-Tyme Concerts held in the parish hall that Mrs. Macdonald participated in and helped to direct. Also the garden parties held on the lawn at the Presbyterian church. The verandah of the manse was the stage for the talent. Mrs. Macdonald was an excellent storyteller. I recall one night when I was in my first year of high school, being in the parish hall in Norval when she told the story of the sinking of the *Marco Polo* ship on the shore of Prince Edward Island. She held the audience enthralled. You could have heard a pin drop as she described the heroic rescue of the sailors from the ship that was battered to pieces on the rocks. They rescued every sailor that night. In my public-speaking class at school I told the *Marco Polo* story and later repeated it to the whole school.

"Mrs. Macdonald taught Sunday school to a class of young boys, and years later I was talking to one of these boys and he said they wouldn't miss Sunday school for anything because she was so good. They looked forward to it each week; she would make the stories so interesting. You had to be awful sick not to go.

"Norval was a beautiful village when Mrs. Macdonald lived here. Her closest neighbours, the MacPhersons, the Websters, and the Gollops across the street, all competed with each other to have the biggest and the most beautiful flower display. Most of the other homes in the village also had pretty flowers. The little village of Norval on the picturesque Credit River, surrounded by the beautiful tree-top groves, could not be beat for magnificent scenery any time of the year."

Isabelle (Mustard) St. John

Isabelle Mustard grew up in Leaskdale. Isabelle's great uncle, John Mustard, was Maud's high school teacher and a friend of the Macdonald family.

Isabelle was just a small girl when the Macdonalds lived in Leaskdale. In fact, Reverend Macdonald baptized Isabelle. She remembers that on his visits to their farm he would bounce Isabelle and her sister Helen on his knees. She also remembers Reverend Macdonald playing tag with them around the Mustard's cherry tree. When Maud came to visit Isabelle's grandmother, Harriet Mustard, she would let the Mustards' cat sit on her lap. When the cat wet her lap one time, Maud didn't make a fuss at all; in fact, she barely blinked an eye, she was that fond of cats. Although Isabelle doesn't have too many memories of the time the Macdonalds lived in Leaskdale, she did meet up with Maud again in Toronto.

Isabelle Mustard St. John.

L.M. Montgomery signed this book using only her married name — a very unusual thing for her to do. She usually signed her books "L.M. Montgomery Macdonald" when they were for friends. This book was given to Isabelle Mustard's family.

Courtesy Isabelle Mustard St. John.

"I was training to be a nurse at Toronto Western Hospital and Mrs. Macdonald gave a talk to the nurse's alumni when I was just a probationer. My mother corresponded with her quite frequently, and I guess she had told Mrs. Macdonald that I would be there at the talk. My mother told me that Mrs. Macdonald was going to speak, and to go. So anyway, when Mrs. Macdonald finished her speech, she said, *Is Isabelle Mustard in the audience?* And here I was, way at the back, and so she started down the aisle and I started up the aisle and she hugged me and kissed me. Then

she asked me if Mr. Macdonald and she came and picked my cousin and me up, would we go to their home for dinner on Riverside Drive? Well, they did. They picked us up and took us up there. This was in about 1938, I guess. We had dinner and I remember she got out her photograph album, but I can't remember what we ate or anything. But I remember the drive, going across Bloor Street from Jane — Mr. Macdonald wasn't a very good driver and Mrs. Macdonald was gripping the handle on the car all the way along." Isabelle laughs at the memory.

"Her sons weren't there but her helper, or maid, was. I have the invitation that she sent to us to go, and I have a letter Mrs. Macdonald wrote when my grandmother died. And when Chester was two or three, Mrs. Macdonald sent my Grandfather Cook a Christmas card and she signed it from Chester. I talked with a girl who did sewing for her, Mary Ross. Mary went and stayed there at the manse and

The letter L.M. Montgomery sent to Isabelle.

Courtesy Isabelle Mustard St. John.

they'd go out driving at night with the horse and buggy. Mary made a lot of Mrs. Macdonald's dresses. She said Mrs. Macdonald liked to chew spruce gum and she would order it from Eaton's.

"I was born in 1917 so I was only nine when she left Leaskdale. She was a very quiet woman and I got the impression that she kept to herself, so I was a bit surprised when she went to the length of hugging and kissing me, years later in Toronto. That was my moment with Lucy Maud," Isabelle says with a laugh.

Eva (Banks) Dalton

Eva Banks was born in 1916, making her only one year younger than Stuart Macdonald. Her family lived in Leaskdale, and even though they were members of Leaskdale's United church, and not of its Presbyterian church, where Reverend Macdonald was the minister, L.M. Montgomery visited the Banks family when the children were ill.

"When we had the measles, Mrs. Macdonald came over. She didn't come in our house, but she came over and asked my mother how we were. There were five of us and we were all sick at the same time, so we were upstairs in bed. It was summertime and the window was up, so we could hear them talking outside. Mrs. Macdonald inquired how we were and if we were coming along all right. She came on behalf of her husband because he was the minister of the Presbyterian church.

"My parents were members of the United church, but we went to public school with most of the kids from the Presbyterian church and they coaxed us to go to Sunday school there with them, so we did. That's when I got to know

Eva Banks Dalton.

Mrs. Macdonald better. She was sort of a sophisticated woman. Her hair was dark, and in those days women nearly all had their hair done up. I know that at Christmastime, sometimes, she would write a play for their concert. I knew her to speak to, but that was pretty well it. I remember dialogue she directed which was for the boys. They all made rooster heads from brown wrapping paper to wear. My brother was in it. [Mrs. Macdonald] wrote it, and I think she must have directed it as well.

"I would have been around Stuart's age. I knew him from school. I had an older brother and Stuart used to love to come over on Saturdays and play in the barn. My father used to be so nervous about them jumping around in the haymow. He was afraid they'd get hurt. Stuart was a lively boy, a nice boy. A good-looking boy, actually. Stuart's older brother, Chester, was more stoutish. I can remember Chester and a boy sitting near him getting into a fight, and they'd get right up and start scrapping right there in school, during school hours. I remember one fellow he scrapped with — Harold Mills was his name. He was about Chester's age.

"Stuart and Chester were both going to public school at the same time I was going there, till they moved away to Norval. I remember one thing, it was kind of a comical thing. Of course, it was a one-room schoolhouse, and I remember when we'd have our lunch hour, if I was eating a cookie, lots of times Stuart would grab my cookie, take a bite, say thank you, and give it back to me [hearty laugh].

Did you know L.M. Montgomery was famous? Had you read any of her books?

"No, I never had any idea. I don't think I had read any at that time. It was after that, that I realized that she was a great writer."

Olive (Harrison) Elliot

Olive Harrison was born in 1917, and her family owned the Leaskdale General Store, where Maud would go for her mail and supplies. Olive's family were members of the Presbyterian church where Reverend Macdonald was the minister, and their house was just a few doors away from the manse, the Macdonalds' home. Although Olive was only nine years old when the Macdonalds left Leaskdale, she has memories of playing at their home.

Do you remember seeing Mrs. Macdonald at church?

"Oh, yes. Mrs. Macdonald sat in the second back seat on the left-hand side of the church, right across from our family. She'd sit and do this [twiddles her thumbs, with hands locked together] all through the service."

Mirroring a scene from her most famous book, Maud rushed to the aid of the Elliot family in much the same way that Anne rushed to help the Barry family in *Anne of Green Gables*. "My brother swallowed Gilt's Lye — that's a poison

A meeting of a literary club in Uxbridge of which Maud was a member, summer 1915, at the home of John Thompson. Maud is in the back row, second from the right, with her arm around a post.

Courtesy Wilda and Harold Clark.

— when he was about three," Olive recalls. "I would have been about seven at the time. Mrs. Macdonald came down to the store right away, as soon as she heard it, and helped him out until they took him to the hospital."

What did she do, exactly?

"Well, she got him vomiting somehow. I don't know what she gave him, exactly. She was a great help. The community always figured she was wonderful then. She was a great friend of mother's."

Did Mrs. Macdonald come over to your home often?

"Well, she was down pretty well every day for the mail, you see. We ran the post office from our store. And I do remember the Macdonalds coming over for a meal."

The Leaskdale General Store as it was when Olive's family ran it. L.M. Montgomery went there daily for her mail. Painting by Allan McGillivray.

Courtesy Isabelle St. John.

Was she friendly, outgoing?

"Yes, very much so. I liked her."

Did you talk to her at all?

"Not too much, because I was so young."

Where was your store located?

"Well, the store burned down several years ago, but if you visit Leaskdale, there's a new store right where it was. It was only a short walk from the Macdonalds' house."

Olive remembers Chester and Stuart well, and even though they were five and two years older respectively, they used to play hide and seek with the little girl.

"There weren't many other kids right around," Olive explains. "My sister was six years older, so she didn't play with me much. Chester and Stuart and I played tag and various other games. I remember going upstairs in the manse and we were up there jumping on the bed. That was only done once, though. I guess we got stopped, likely. They always had hired help. And I remember that hammock on their verandah. I really liked that. I'd rock in it. I always wanted one, but I never got one."

Olive Elliot

Courtesy Nina Elliot.

Eleanor Dawson

Eleanor Dawson was a fellow parishioner of Maud's at the Victoria Presbyterian Church in Toronto, nearby Maud's home on Riverside Drive.

"When I was growing up, I lived in the west end of Toronto. I went to Victoria Presbyterian Church. Mrs. Montgomery [Macdonald] was a member there. I used to see her every Sunday. The pictures you see of her with her pince nez glasses and her big hat and her hair like a Gibson girl, that's how she looked to me; that's how I remember her. I was a big fan of hers from away back and I'd read all her books. We just talked and chatted about, you know, everyday things. She was most pleasant. She told me, *Now you bring your book, and I'll sign it,* but I kept forgetting every Sunday. So I never did get it signed but she was such a pleasant lady."

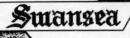

Mrs. R. C. Smith
Chairman 1919 - 39

To Mrs. R. C. Smith

Started with a few borrowed books

On behalf of the Council of Swansea and the members of the Library Board of the village, we desire you to accept these volumes, on your retirement from the chairmanship of the Library Board, after twenty years' of most faithful and devoted interest in prompting good and wholesome reading in the homes of the citizens.

Under your wise leadership, the Library was created as a memorial to the soldiers of Swansea who sacrificed their lives in the Great War. No more precious and practical memorial could be erected than that of a library of good books. You have watched it grow from small beginnings to occupy a real place in the life of the community: may your dream of a permanent and beautiful home for the Library be realized in the years of your retirement.

Has now more than Six thousand volumes

The Library will always reflect the interest you displayed in creating high thoughts and mental enjoyment in the lives of young and old. As you pass on your duties to others, may they catch something of your spirit, and emulate you in your faithfulness and interest.

These volumes carry to you, in your hours of ease and quiet, the sincere appreciation of those closely associated with you in your labours of love, and also the appreciation of that large number of the people of the village who have found in the Library a source of enjoyment and inspiration.

Edgar Jermany.
CHAIRMAN OF THE LIBRARY BOARD

C. C. Down
REEVE

F. Metcalf
DPT. REEVE

L. M. Montgomery Macdonald
N. C. Lane

Maud remained active in her community even after she and her husband retired. As evident here on this 1939 Swansea Memorial Library document, Maud was a member of the library board — her signature is at the bottom.

Courtesy Norm McLeod.

Chapter Four
Mrs. Macdonald, Our Sunday School Teacher

A regular churchgoer in her youth, Maud had taught Sunday school in
Cavendish and had also played the organ. When she became a minister's wife,
she was well equipped to fulfil the duties that her husband's congregation
expected of her. Not only did she teach Sunday school, but she organized and
directed plays and concerts within the Young People's groups of the
Presbyterian churches. Well organized and well read, she always had sugges-
tions about which plays, songs, and skits would be most appropriate and
enjoyable for the community. She sometimes even wrote the skits herself.
Maud came up with the idea of having Old-Tyme Concerts in Norval, and she
organized a committee to stage these events. The productions featured vaude-

ville-style entertainment presented by adult members of the community dressed up in old-fashioned clothing.

L.M. Montgomery.

Courtesy Prince Edward Island Archives and Records Office.

Margaret (Macdonald) McKane

Mrs. McKane lives just three houses west of Union Presbyterian Church, one of the two churches that were under Reverend Macdonald's charge while he was in Norval, Ontario. A former member of the Young People's Society, Margaret Macdonald was born March 21, 1915. She was eleven when the Macdonalds came to live in Norval and twenty when they left. A very energetic and upbeat person, Mrs. McKane gives talks to groups interested in hearing about L.M. Montgomery and the Macdonalds' connection to Union church and Norval.

"L.M. Montgomery was very dear to my heart. Her husband, the Reverend Macdonald, was the minister of the Norval Presbyterian Church, and also Union Presbyterian Church, and I joined the church while he was here. The two churches are about the same size; we jointly contribute to the minister's salary and the upkeep. Reverend Macdonald was a very jovial person, very warm-hearted and so fatherly. All my memories of him are very pleasant. At that time, the Macdonalds did have a car, but they sometimes drove here in a horse and buggy; the horse's name was Queen. The Macdonalds also would visit with different people from the two churches. Our farm was just a couple of miles across from Union church, and at the next farm there was a man who weighed 350 pounds. He couldn't go to church, but the Macdonalds would often go to visit him. At the time they were here, there was one service in the morning and the other in the afternoon. One year, Norval would have the morning service and the next year, it would be Union.

"Our Young People's Society had folded prior to their arrival. When Mrs. Macdonald came here, she resurrected it and made it into a drama club. She coached us and we went all over the countryside putting on plays to raise funds for the church. She was just one of us. We didn't think of her as a 'very important person,' we just knew her as our minister's wife. The young people got to know her very well, going to meetings and play practices. I could go to her and ask her anything.

"I can remember once, she said, *We're going to Morristown to put on a play*. I said, *Oh, I can't go. I'm on the committee for the dance at the high school that night*. So she changed the date. That's the way she was; she did those kinds of things. I had a role in one or two of the plays and was the lead in one that was called *Jane*. My husband [to-be] was also a member of the Young People's, and he would carry the props and help set up. Mrs. Macdonald was good at directing. She knew exactly what she wanted and how she was going to do it. It was so much fun and we all had a good time. We just loved her, and Mr. Macdonald would come to the meetings, too; he would sit at the back and wait for her.

"She was also a member of the Women's Missionary Society that met once a month, and she used to take her turn, giving readings in her home. She was always very regal looking. She would sit there very daintily and she had a lorgnette. A dressmaker made her clothing, and her jewellery was beautiful. Her hair was always just perfect. She was very pleasant to be around, and if you asked, she would give her opinion. If you ever wanted her to come and give a reading or a monologue or take part in some way for a good cause, she would do it. When in 1933 we celebrated the hundredth anniversary of Union church, we had a book published to commemorate it and she edited the book herself.

"Even after she retired and went to live in Toronto, she came back here to visit in the house just beside the church and spent the afternoon. But her cat was sick and she'd left him with a sitter, so she couldn't stay too late because she wanted to get back to her cat. Her son Stuart said she would get up very early to do her writing, and in the evenings she would read. She was an avid reader. She loved to do so many things. She enjoyed cooking, she sewed well, she did needlework, and she loved flowers. Stuart was so much like his mother. He was

Margaret Macdonald McKane with the portrait of L.M. Montgomery that hangs in the Union church

a very handsome boy, and quite an athlete. One year, I think it was 1932 ... he won the Junior Ontario Gymnastics Award and [he won] the National Junior Gymnastics Award in 1933. He was a top-notch person. Stuart went with a girl down in Norval, a really nice girl who never married. When he went to university, he met somebody else. Those boys, both Stuart and Chester, were a delight to Mrs. Macdonald.

"I have given so many talks on L.M. Montgomery. I've had busloads come here. For three or four years, tenth graders from Etobicoke have come. They come to the church, two busloads a day for three days, to get a talk on Union church and the history of the area and L.M. Montgomery. I also had a busload of senior citizens who went to Norval church to see the plaque [dedicated to Reverend Macdonald and L.M. Montgomery] and then they came to Union

1833   CENTENNIAL   1933

The Union church's hundredth-anniversary booklet, which L.M. Montgomery edited in 1933.

Courtesy Margaret Macdonald McKane.

church. Many people have never heard of Union church; they don't realize that L.M. Montgomery was also here as the minister's wife.

"I remember after the Macdonalds retired, they went and lived on the Humber River in Toronto and Mrs. Macdonald would invite some of the ladies from the church to spend the afternoon. My mother drove our car and took a load of the ladies there. Mrs. Macdonald was so generous and we always saw the happy side of her. The last couple of years that they were here, Reverend Macdonald was not well and we had some substitute ministers. I know it was hard for her but it was marvellous how she managed. When they left, there was a great write-up about her that I cut out. I have several clippings written about her throughout the years.

"I know she respected and admired her husband. You felt that by the way she spoke to him, and of him. Marriage isn't always what you think it's going to be and we all have our ups and downs. We have to be thankful for what joy we are given. I feel that she had much joy and much happiness.

"When some people who never even knew her came out to Norval church several years ago and gave a talk about what a terrible life she'd had, I had to leave. I couldn't sit through it. Because the woman I knew wasn't the woman they were talking about. I know she had a great deal to put up with, being the minister's wife and all the adversity she had, and maybe things didn't always go the way she wanted [them] to, but she had so much happiness. L.M. Montgomery was a wonderful person. She was a great lady who did marvellous things. She gave so much happiness to so many people."

Craig Reid

Craig Reid, known as "Red Craig" when he was a youngster because of his bright red hair, lived two and a half miles from Norval, but made the one-hour hike every day to attend school. Luella Reid, Chester Macdonald's first wife and the mother of L.M. Montgomery's grandchildren, Luella and Cameron, is Craig's first cousin. The oldest of five, Craig attended Sunday school at Norval's Presbyterian church and especially enjoyed L.M. Montgomery's Bible class.

"When the Macdonalds came to Norval in 1926, I was in junior Sunday school, but as we moved up and became about thirteen or fourteen years old, we generally went into Mrs. Macdonald's class. She taught what we called Senior Boys and it was quite interesting. You got into a different level as well as a different attitude of the verses and catechisms than we'd heard and read in the junior classes. Mrs. Macdonald explained the different books of the Bible. She would have a course and it would maybe take a month to study the whole book she chose. She explained things as we went along and gave us a different outlook on life. She was quite good at asking questions to get our ideas and thoughts as she went along on the different subjects. Oh, she

Craig Reid (second from right in the front) and his family, February 1928.

Courtesy Craig Reid.

had young *men* in that class, that's how interesting it was. They were eighteen and nineteen years of age."

Do you remember anything specific that you learned in that class?

"[One] of the things that she talked about was the way we lived in those days compared to how they lived back in the first part of the Bible. She brought out the idea that how we were living more or less set our thoughts on what you should do and what you shouldn't do; and what you were interested in. I was a farmer's son and I was quite interested in growing the different grains and raising livestock. She would ask us to compare our ideas to those in the Bible. This was what the young fellows got a kick out of — her imagination. She could take subjects out of the Bible and make plays of them. Mrs. Macdonald studied plays that were written by different authors, too, and she would put an extra actor or two in it. Her plays went over very well with the community. They'd do the play at Norval and then take it to Union. They raised considerable money doing that. The church had to raise money because about 1929 was the stock market crash and in the early 1930s was the Great Depression. I know she coached two or three plays that raised funds to help carry on and pay towards the Sunday school. Mrs. Macdonald had a very clear voice when she was explaining something. She talked very quickly, but she was very clear and she could hold a person's attention. When she was in a crowd or a group, she could talk and get their attention and that made so much difference."

Do you remember what the plays were?

"I can't remember the names of the plays, but I know one was about an older couple living in the Depression and how the young people tried to get them moving on to different things and they couldn't afford it. It was very depressing, pretty much all the way through. Another thing they had in Norval was a concert that brought in all the older songs from the 1910s through into the 1930s. They didn't have that only within the Norval Presbyterian Church; there were United Church members in it as well as the Anglican Church. All three churches went together to have this concert and that went over very well, the singing.

"I don't think I ever enjoyed plays as much as I did when Mrs. Macdonald was involved in the coaching of them and the teaching of them. One evening Mrs. Macdonald was putting on a play up at Union church. My uncle Robert Reid was going with his two boys and daughter Luella. I wanted to go, but our family had no money to spare. The entrance was twenty-five cents per person and we just didn't have it. That afternoon, our cousin Reverend Joe Reid and his wife came out to our place from Toronto. His wife was admiring a milk stool I'd made that had won second prize at the school fair. She said, *You know, Craig, I'd love to have something like that for a footstool when I'm reading. Would you make me one?* Dad said, *You wouldn't want one quite that high.* So we made another stool that afternoon and she took it back to Toronto with her. She gave me fifty cents for making this stool. I said to my dad, *I've got fifty cents now; there's two of us* [my brother Weir and I]. *We can go.* So we called my Uncle Rob and got a ride with him to see Mrs. Macdonald's play."

Did you know Stuart? Were you about the same age as he was?

"Yes. Stuart was born in 1915 and I was born in 1916, and he was a little bit ahead of me in school. He was also a bit smarter. [Laughs.] He was a smart boy, gosh, he could pretty well turn his hands to anything. He was quite interesting to play around with and chum with while we went to public school. He was inclined to be quite a character in a way. He could get into mischief as well as any of us, in fact more so, I think. I can remember when we went to church one Sunday, the young devil started at the front of the church from their seat in the third pew on the side and crawled all the way down the full length of church underneath the pews, and I thought, well, what a thing to do. He would have been about twelve or thirteen. Anything to create some action, he would do it. Stuart was quite active in sports; he was a good swimmer and he liked baseball. I didn't get to know Chester very well until later. He married my cousin and they had two children."

What sort of a preacher was Reverend Macdonald?

"When he first came, he wasn't bad. At the Sunday school level, he used to have a question period after we had been in the classes. That was quite inter-esting. I had a brother who used to be the top guy in answering the questions. He was just a corker at that. The rest of us would just be sort of dumbfounded, the things that he would come out with in answer to what Reverend Macdonald asked. But as far as his services, the first three or four years were quite interesting and he held a fairly good attendance, but then he started to drift away. I understand that Mrs. Macdonald had to help him a lot in the last three years he was there [when his illness progressed]."

How did Mrs. Macdonald dress?

"She was always very elegantly dressed. I can see Mrs. Macdonald going down for the mail every day to the Norval post office, always at about one o'clock or so,

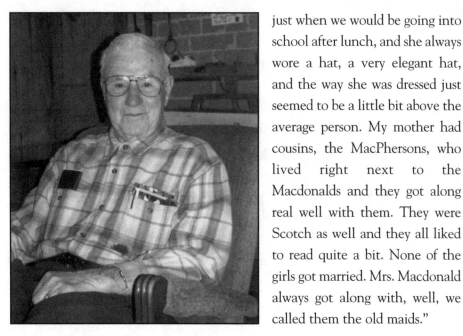

"Red" Craig Reid today.

just when we would be going into school after lunch, and she always wore a hat, a very elegant hat, and the way she was dressed just seemed to be a little bit above the average person. My mother had cousins, the MacPhersons, who lived right next to the Macdonalds and they got along real well with them. They were Scotch as well and they all liked to read quite a bit. None of the girls got married. Mrs. Macdonald always got along with, well, we called them the old maids."

Did you ever have occasion to go to the Macdonalds' home?

"Oh, yes. For Sunday school concerts at Christmas, we'd go to their home for practices. We had dialogues and she, with one or two other ladies, would instruct the whole Sunday school to make this concert up for Christmas. She didn't teach singing; there was another lady there who was quite musical and would teach all the different carols and we'd sing them. But Mrs. Macdonald took charge of the dialogues and she would write some of them, too. We had the 'March of the Wooden Soldiers' [laughs]. We'd march and go around and then when you finished that march, you were all dead and you fell down. The captain would push you all off and you'd all go that way off the stage. Mrs. Macdonald directed a lot of those things. She recited a lot of papers and poems that she'd written, and it was quite interesting. She had poems that brought in the Christmas spirit. Here again, she would ad lib in some of the poems, which made it quite interesting. She was an excellent speaker. She had a good voice and it carried really well, too. You could hear her over quite an audience and you'd have no trouble hearing her at the back. Her voice just seemed to carry, while you get some people who just sort of talk and it drops right in front of them, but not Mrs. Macdonald."

Do you remember anything about her appearance?

"Her hands. I know she used to use her hands a fair amount. She also wore jewellery which we thought in those days was quite the thing. She wore glasses and I can remember her having a set of glasses with a leg on, that she could put up on her nose for reading and then take it off. Her hair was brushed back in a bun. When I first remember, it was very dark, a blackish brown. Then about three or four years later, it started to grey."

When Mrs. Macdonald arrived in Norval, did you know that she was famous?

"No, no we didn't. This is something that I think was just quite an asset to the congregation, that she was a writer and a reader, and the more they got to know her, the higher the esteem they felt for her. People were interested in having her speak. When the princes came to Canada, she was presented to them. The way I remember her, she always seemed to be more or less a happy person."

Jean (Giffen) Macdonald

Born December 13, 1911, Jean Giffen was fourteen years old when L.M. Montgomery moved to Norval. The youngest of five children, Jean grew up on a farm and was a member of the Norval Presbyterian Church where Reverend Macdonald was the minister for nine years.

"We used to sometimes be at Mrs. Macdonald's place, the big brick manse right next to the church, for Young People's meetings, and she would talk to us. She had a cat who would come and wind around our legs, rubbing up against them, and he seemed really friendly. But then when we would put out a hand to pet him, he would go, *Pssst!* And scratch at you! We would study from the Bible, and she would instruct us. She would sometimes tell us stories that would later appear in her books.

"We invited the Macdonalds to our wedding on October 17, 1934, at my father's house. My first cousin was a minister and he performed the ceremony, but we wanted to invite Reverend Macdonald because he'd been our minister for so many years in Norval. Reverend Macdonald was full of fun, full of jokes. He liked to tease just about anybody."

Reverend Macdonald gave a toast to Jean at the reception and pronounced the benediction. Jean remembers: "Mrs. Macdonald was more reserved than her husband. Reverend Macdonald was a very good minister and gave good sermons."

Jean knew that L.M. Montgomery was a famous writer, and although she'd read many of her books, including her personal

Jean Giffen Macdonald.

favourite, *Anne of Green Gables*, before the Macdonalds arrived in Norval, Jean never spoke to Maud about her books. "I was too shy," she admits.

Claude McLaughlin

When the Macdonalds left Norval, the Young People's Society and L.M. Montgomery's Bible class got together and presented Maud and Ewan with a glass relish plate on a silver tray. Claude McLaughlin, who was twenty-three at the time, was chosen to make the presentation.

"I was in her Sunday school class for about three years. Mrs. Macdonald said she liked teaching young guys like myself — I was a teenager at that time — because we would ask questions. She said the girls wouldn't ask any questions.

"Mrs. Macdonald could just talk about anything. I remember once when we had the Young People's Society at the church and we had a debate. They had a couple of lawyers there as judges. Gordon Green, a Brampton lawyer and member of Parliament for Peel, was there at the Sunday school that night to be one of the judges at the debate. One thing led to another and he pulled a joke on Mrs. Macdonald, so she turned around and got one on him [by telling a joke about lawyers]. She said, *You know, Abraham Lincoln wasn't a very handsome* man. *One cold winter day he arrived in a town where he'd been hired to act as a lawyer, and when he got to the courthouse, there were a lot of other lawyers all crowded around the stove, keeping warm. Somebody said to him, 'You just look as if you came from that place we don't mention very often [Hell].' And he said, 'Yes, exactly. That's where I came from.' And this other lawyer said, 'Well, how did you find it there?' 'Well,' he said, 'just like it is here. There were so many lawyers around I couldn't get near the fire.' And boy, they got a laugh out of that.*

"Mrs. Macdonald wrote a lot of the plays and skits that we put on in Norval. They always had a big play that they put on in the parish hall in Norval. Oh boy, that place would just be jammed to the doors. She was popular. She seemed to draw people to her. You might see some people who were famous like her and they'd look down their nose at you. But she wouldn't do that. You know, when they had those fowl suppers in the church, Mrs. Macdonald wouldn't be out there greeting people. She'd be helping the ladies in the kitchen wash the dishes."

Did you know either of the boys?

"Oh, yes. I knew Chester maybe better. He was a little younger than I was. We had fowl suppers in the church in those days to raise some money. I remember sitting beside him and he had some carrots on his plate. He'd been mulling around through them with his fork and I could see he didn't like them. He said to me, *Do you like carrots?* I said, *Oh, yes, I like carrots.* So he got his plate and scraped them off onto my plate — after he'd been mulling through them! The other boy, Stuart, was quite a smart lad. Both the boys went to St. Andrew's College. Stuart wanted to go into medicine. He had been picking things up pretty easily. But the first year in university, he failed. So he got a summer job at the Campbell Soup Factory, doing manual labour. You know, that was the first job he ever had in his life. When he came home that night, he went straight to bed, he was that tired. Anyway, he went back to university the next year and he eventually ended up a doctor. Not only a doctor, but a specialist. He was a sur-

Claude McLaughlin.

geon at the Wellesley Hospital in Toronto. You know, if anyone from Norval went into the hospital, he'd go and see them. He was a nice friendly fellow."

Do you remember any of Reverend Macdonald's sermons?

"Oh yes. He was a good preacher. Mrs. Macdonald sat just across the aisle from where we sat, three-quarters of the way to the front. She sat there alone most of the time because her boys were away at school. She'd sit there and pay attention to the minister, with her hands folded in her lap. She looked right at home there, and I think she liked it in Norval, because it was a handy place to get to Toronto from. I don't think she drove, though. Reverend Macdonald always drove the car, I know that. Anyway, we got to know her, and no matter who you were, she'd have a word with you.

"When they lived in Norval, they had a Willys-Knight car. You don't see any of those now. They had the sleeve-valve engines in them and they wouldn't start in the wintertime. So they put it in the garage and jacked it up and it stayed in there all winter."

Did the Macdonalds have a good relationship?

"Oh, I think so. I think they got along alright. As far as I know."

Did you ever go to her house for any reason?

"Well, we went to her house to practise a play. We generally went around from house to house. She was a person people liked. They liked her and she was a good-looking woman."

Did she ever come to your house?

"Oh, yes, she'd come to the house, she and Reverend Macdonald, and stay for supper sometimes."

Did she tell stories?

"No, she was just like the rest of us, talked about current events and things going on in the neighbourhood."

Did you know she was famous?

"Oh, yes, she was famous when she came here. We knew that."

Had you read any of her books?

"Oh, yes. I read *Anne of Green Gables* first, and I liked that book. A lot of those books were written right in Norval in the manse there.

"Mrs. Macdonald wasn't a person who would look down her nose at you. She greeted everybody. She was at home with paupers or with a king. She could meet anybody."

Ruth (Giffen) Forgrave

Ruth Giffen was greatly influenced by meeting L.M. Montgomery. As a teacher, she introduced many students to Anne of Green Gables.

"My personal memories of Lucy Maud are from the time when they were living in Norval. Reverend Macdonald was the minister of the Norval Presbyterian Church and Union Presbyterian Church. At that time, I happened to have a boyfriend who went to the Union church, and he was in the plays that Maud used to conduct. I used to be at some of the play practices, you see, and that's how I saw her in action with the young people. I remember her as a very gracious lady. She held her head well up and kind of to the side. It would shake every once in a while. She loved to dress up and look smart. In those days not as many people wore earrings and that sort of thing as they do now, but I picture her with these hanging earrings and she liked to wear hats with feathers and flowers. She was the epitome of what a minister's wife was expected to be. Teaching Sunday school, helping with the Young People's, going to the ladies meetings. Her first book, *Anne of Green Gables*, is a treasure. It's just a beautiful story. You can read it and reread it."

Did you read it when you knew her or later?

"I read it later. I hadn't read any of her books when I met her."

Ruth Forgrave with the book she loaned out to her students as a special treat.

Ruth taught grade four for many years before retiring in 1971. "*Anne of Green Gables* was just right for the end of the year. I had a special edition, which I allowed the children to take home for one night so they could have it all to themselves. I still have it. It's out of print now, but it's beautifully illustrated, and this was a very great privilege for them to be able to take it home. I read a passage from *Anne of Green Gables* every day to the children. Matthew made me think of my own father." Ruth has become so familiar with the book that she can quote passages from it, word for word. "L.M. Montgomery had a marvellous way with words. *Anne of Green Gables* really touched me. This was a very human story and she was very knowledgeable of the feelings of the human being. My husband took me to Prince Edward Island, and he was so thrilled to have me there because he knew how much I loved this book. You wouldn't believe the number of postcards I've received from Green Gables from former students writing to tell me they were there."

Did you ever talk to L.M. Montgomery?

"Oh, yes, I spoke with her, but I can't remember exactly what about. The Norval people were very proud to have her as their minister's wife. I attended Union church sometimes with friends, when I was visiting there for the weekend. Mr. Macdonald was a nice old guy, I liked him. He had a dry humour, you know, greeting people and shaking hands with them at the door. I just thought of Mrs. Macdonald as a perfect minister's wife. Always on hand, always supporting her husband. We don't get that today, you know. Mrs. Macdonald was a very hardworking woman. She loved giving readings. They had a social tea at the church and she gave a reading. I knew her older son, Chester. They used to have what you call garden parties — mostly the churches and some other charitable organizations. It was a money-raising affair that was held at somebody's home that had a nice garden. And chairs were brought in, they had a platform built, and so on. They would bring in quite good talent to entertain. Well, this particular time when the Macdonalds were in Norval, it was held on the manse grounds. I can remember being there and seeing Chester and Luella. They were boyfriend and girlfriend. I knew Luella; I went to high school with her.

"I remember Mrs. Macdonald as a very gracious lady and one who was willing to put up with the young people and all their cavorting around. They did three or four plays under her direction while she was here."

Jim Clark

Jim Clark lived on a farm outside of Norval, and because the Clark family regularly attended services at Norval's Presbyterian church, Jim was acquainted with L.M. Montgomery as Mrs. Macdonald, the minister's wife.

Jim took part in some of the plays that Mrs. Macdonald directed, but doesn't remember his part in them very well. "I think I forgot one of my lines, but I just went on to the next one. It didn't seem to matter very much," he remembers with a laugh. He thought L.M. Montgomery was "a very nice lady and always well dressed. I think she liked Norval — it was a pretty village."

Jim remembers that Reverend Macdonald was enthusiastically welcomed by the Norval congregation. "Mr. Patterson was the minister before Reverend Macdonald. He was Irish and had a quick temper. Reverend Macdonald was a good successor because he was more moderate in his preaching."

Jim Clark

Courtesy Jim Clark.

After the service, the congregation would meet in the basement, and Reverend Macdonald would talk to the parishioners and shake their hands. Jim remembers L.M. Montgomery as being very active in the church. "Mrs. Macdonald was the overall director of the Sunday school and Christmas concerts and delegated different areas to other people."

Jim admits he didn't realize at the time how famous the minister's wife was, but says, "We knew she was well educated."

A postcard Maud made of a clipping of her favourite cat Lucky, to give to friends.

Courtesy Jim Clark.

L. M. Montgomery's favorite cat, Good Luck, who is one of the Characters in "The Blue Castle".

L. M. Montgomery

L. M. Montgomery was born at Clifton, Prince Edward Island and spent her childhood days in the seashore farming settlement of Cavendish, which is the setting of many of her stories. Although still known to her readers as "L. M. Montgomery" she has for some years presided over a Presbyterian Manse in Ontario, for she is the wife of the Reverend Ewan Macdonald.

Chapter Five
L.M. Montgomery, Famous Author

Maud was grateful and happy for her success, and she loved being famous. Every fan letter she received was answered with a handwritten letter. When young fans phoned Maud at her home, she graciously spoke with them — she was never rude or impatient about having been disturbed at home. She granted interviews to anyone who requested one, even schoolgirls writing for their school paper. Many organizations, big and small, asked her to come and speak to their group. She complied as often as she could. L.M. Montgomery was a person with a big heart — she was generous with her time, even though she often had so little to spare.

A photographic
portrait of Maud
taken at around
the time *Anne of
Green Gables* was
published.

*Courtesy Prince Edward
Island Public Archives
and Records Office.*

Bernice (Thurman) Hunter

As a child growing up during the Depression, Bernice Thurman idolized L.M. Montgomery. Her fondest wish was to be a writer just like Montgomery. She hasn't forgotten the day she was lucky enough to be invited to afternoon tea at Maud's and have the famous author critique her work.

In the mid-1930s, when Bernice Thurman heard that her favourite author, L.M. Montgomery, had moved into her neighbourhood of Swansea in west Toronto, she was thrilled. At fourteen, Bernice had already decided that she was going to be a writer.

Inquisitive and highly motivated in her determination to begin her career, Bernice eagerly looked up Maud's phone number in the Toronto phone book. "I talked to her on the phone a couple of times. I'd call her up and she'd answer. I was always, always trying to get hints about how to be a writer like her, and she was always kind and nice."

Bernice Thurman Hunter today.

Bernice also wrote to Maud asking for advice on how to get started as a writer, and Maud graciously replied in a four-page handwritten letter dated July 12, 1937: "You ask if you are too young to be writing a book. If you mean writing a book with the expectation of publishing, I would say emphatically much much too young. I cannot think any girl of fourteen, no matter how earnest and gifted she might be, could possibly write a book which any publisher would accept. But if you mean writing a book for your own pleasure and for training in the art of expression and creation then age has nothing to do with it. It will be good practice for you." She answered each of Bernice's questions, going on to say, "Do not ever consider your writing more important than your studies. Nobody needs a good education more than a would-be writer ... You have chosen a very interesting but a very exacting career ... if you have talent and perseverance you will succeed in the end." Maud's words proved to be prophetic.

In September 1937, when Bernice began her first year of high school, she met a girl who lived on Riverside Drive. "She was out of my class. But we had one thing in common. We both loved reading. So we happened to be eating lunch together and discussing our favourite authors. I mentioned that L.M. Montgomery was my favourite author and she said, *Oh, that's Mrs. Macdonald, she's our neighbour.* And of course I couldn't believe it. Imagine, she was actually living next door to my idol. *I can probably get us an invitation*, she said. Sure enough, the next day she came back and said, *We're invited to afternoon tea on Saturday.*

"My mother got all excited because she loved L.M. Montgomery's books too. *Oh, you're going to meet this grand lady,* she worried, *and you don't have proper clothes.* Then she pressed my skirt, darned my sweater, and turned the collar and cuffs of my white blouse, and I looked very presentable. Under my arm I carried my workbook with my latest story carefully penned inside."

What was she like? She seems so full of humour in her books.

"She definitely didn't joke with us or anything like that. A lady who worked for her came out with a tray loaded with green-cheese pinwheel sandwiches. I'd never seen green cheese in my life before. And there were little cakes covered with pink icing that cracked when you bit into them. We had our tea in the backyard. We never went into the house. We went down the driveway, which had little white stones all over it, then down two steps into the backyard. There was red wooden garden furniture out there and big trees. She showed us the grave of her little cat. Behind the yard was the Humber River.

"Anyway, she read a few pages of my workbook and said I must remember that a writer had to have higher education, that you couldn't hope to be published unless you were a university graduate. You needed higher education, more than high school, she said. And in those days, and particularly in my class of people, you were very lucky to stay in high school until you graduated with a diploma because it got you a job. So my mum considered that we were very well educated. Lots of people didn't keep their kids in high school. Lots of people made their kids stop at the age of fourteen to go to work to help the family. My mother knew that education was the key. But higher education — that was beyond us.

Bernice with her aunt, Alice Thurman, in the 1930s.

Courtesy Bernice Thurman Hunter.

"My older sister should have gone to university, but there just wasn't the money and in those days there were no scholarships to be had to help you with your education. When L.M. Montgomery told me that I must have higher education, I can still feel my heart dropping because I knew that I wasn't going to get this 'higher education' and so I felt defeated. And yet she'd said two very good things: she said I had a good imagination — which was a lovely thing to hear. And she said the most important thing of all, *Your characters ring true.* When I got home, I wrote that phrase down so I would never forget it. So those were encouraging words. But then I'd remember the discouraging words — *You must remember, Bernice, that you must have a good education to be a writer.* Well, I just gave up the idea of being a writer then. But that doesn't stop you from writing when you love to write. So that's why I just kept on."

Was L.M. Montgomery your favourite author?

"Oh, heavens yes. And you read her books not once, but every one over and over and over. I couldn't even tell you how many times I've read every one of her books. You never get tired of them."

How did you get to be a writer? When did you begin to have your work published?

"One year, Alexander Ross, who wrote a column for the *Toronto Telegram* asked people to write in and fill his column while he was on holidays. I wrote a column and was paid fifty dollars. That was my first cheque. The column was called "A Grandchild Can Make Life Beautiful Again." I was forty-nine years old. I just wrote a description about my first grandchild and what she meant in my life. Alexander Ross was kind enough to say, *This was the most beautiful description of a baby I have read anytime, anywhere. Keep writing.* Those words coming from an author encouraged me. And that helped me to keep writing."

Bernice began to write short stories and had several published in school readers and children's magazines. Then she started writing what would become her first published book, *That Scatterbrain Booky*. "I was looking for material to write a story. I thought, well, some interesting things happened when we were kids, why don't I write about it? So I started writing *That Scatterbrain Booky*, only I didn't know it would become a book. Once I started writing about my childhood, the memories just started flooding back. So I continued and typed it up and edited the best I could and sent it to a publisher. It was only a short time later when the president of Scholastic Canada phoned me himself and said, *I want to be the first to tell you that we're going to publish your book*."

Did you ever hear anymore about L.M. Montgomery after the day you met her? Were you aware when she died?

"Well, I remember reading it in the paper and just being knocked out by it. They had a picture of her on the front page. It was very shocking. I didn't know at that time that she died at what we now consider an early age. I was so young, I thought she was quite old. I know now how young she was [sixty-seven]. But I'm not pretending I knew her like a friend or anything. I met her once and talked to her on the phone a couple of times and she answered my letter. But she had a big influence on my life, because I wanted to be a writer like her."

The funeral of L.M. Montgomery in Cavendish, P.E.I., 1942.

Courtesy National Archives of Canada.

Linda (Olive Watson) Sparks

Olive Watson was fourteen years old and living in the same area of Toronto as L.M. Montgomery when she met the author for the first time. Already a huge fan of Montgomery's, Linda was thrilled when Maud was invited to speak to the women's group at Farmer Memorial Baptist Church, where Linda and her family were members of the congregation. Although her name at the time was Olive, in the early 1940s her friends decided to call her Linda (which had the same initial as her middle name, Lillian). Olive didn't mind. "It seemed like an Anne-like thing to do, to change my name. My friends did it for fun, but then it just stayed with me."

"L.M. Montgomery was most gracious, but you know, just coming in to speak, you're not going to be friendly and chat with everybody. She had grey hair and glasses with a chain or post hanging down from them. She was dressed in sombre colours, but then, older women wore dark colours back then. I seem to remember her outfit was a nice, soft grey. The dress was kind of long, but then in the late 1930s, women of that age were still wearing fairly long dresses. She wore matching gloves. There was a little bit of humour in what she was saying. But I was just thoroughly struck by the fact that 'Here she is!'

"My mother had a first edition of *Anne of Avonlea*, and I had been ferociously reading books since I was ten or so. By the time I was twelve I'd read as many of L.M. Montgomery's books as I could find." Linda recalls with a laugh, "I remember one evening, my girlfriend [who also loved the Anne books] and I sat outside in the backyard and we named all the trees. Because that's what Anne did. Of course, nowadays girls wouldn't do that sort of thing. I also loved the Emily books, because she wanted to be a writer."

When she came to visit your church, did you know Montgomery was a famous author?

"Oh, yes. And so famous that I just couldn't imagine her coming to our church. And to find her very human was incredibly eye-opening to me. I mean, she was human, she was like us, she was like my mother. In my mind's eye, I can still see her. She wore a hat and she was 'properly' dressed. She wore the right things, things that would please my grandmother and my aunts. I can even remember the dress *I* wore that evening. I don't think I would have spoken to her, I was too shy. I may have said hello, but not a conversation. That was just beyond what I could have imagined."

Olive Watson's church group, circa 1939. Olive is in the back row, second from left, and Anita Webb is next to her, in the middle.

Courtesy Reverend Linda Sparks.

Anita Webb, a young cousin of Maud's, came to live with the Macdonalds at their home on Riverside Drive, to help out as a housekeeper and companion. Anita began attending Farmer Memorial Baptist Church, and she and Linda struck up a friendship. "I think she came to our church because it was nearby and she found friends there. Anita was older than I was, and there was another girl there who also became quite close friends with Anita. In the picture, both are wearing hats. We younger girls didn't wear hats. Anita and I took a shine to each other. We were both interested in books. Some people think Green Gables was L.M. Montgomery's home, but it wasn't, it was Anita's family's home. When Anita went back for a visit, she sent me a postcard of the house which I saved."

In April 1938 or 1939 Linda's Sunday school class planned to put on a wedding pageant featuring period wedding dresses. Because Linda was so tiny, Anita asked her if she would like to wear Maud's wedding dress in the pageant. "I was very proud to be asked. Here was a person who I thought was next to God and I was going to be wearing her dress! It had a very tiny waist and I fit into it, but to make sure that nothing would happen, I practically starved myself until the time of the pageant. I was five foot three and three-quarters and the dress was the right length. L.M. Montgomery gave the impression of being a tall person; she carried herself so regally, but she was really only about my height. L.M. Montgomery came to the pageant and she said to me afterwards, *My dear, you walked the best of any of them*. And I thought, 'Well, I couldn't do anything else.' There were stays that held my head up; there were stays around the middle to keep my waist straight. I couldn't bend over; I couldn't slouch. But I was so proud to wear it, and it was because of that event that she was sort of interested in me."

Did you ever go to the Macdonalds' house on Riverside Drive?

"Yes, I did. Later that year, Anita invited me there for supper. There was one son there as well. I think it was Chester. He seemed to me a big man. I was so shy and had always been taught that you speak when you're spoken to. So I didn't think I could initiate anything. It was kind of a quiet dinner. L.M. Montgomery spoke a few times. But I had a feeling there was something else going on. They were bothered about something."

Was Reverend Macdonald there?

"No. I think maybe he was in the hospital. There was no mention of him. Even Anita never talked about him, that I can recall. I was in my teens and I was overawed. I thought so much of L.M. Montgomery's books. I just loved them, and I never thought I'd ever meet her. I was horribly shy and wished someone would say something so that I could say something, too. I was hoping she would talk about Anne, because the characters were like real people to me. I wanted to ask what it was like to write books like that. I loved *The Story Girl*, and one of my very favourites was *A Tangled Web*. I loved how she got all those stories interwoven and then brought it all together in the end. I loved Emily from *Emily of New Moon* because she was always writing her thoughts down. Because of that, I decided I'd have a diary and I would do the same. I wanted to tell L.M. Montgomery that, but she didn't give me an opening. I felt something was brooding. I know Anita wouldn't have asked me for dinner if she'd thought it would be like that. No one was at ease. I certainly wasn't. There was something going on. I wondered why she didn't ask me about myself or somehow give me an opening to start a conversation.

"It was a fairly large table. Her son sat across from me and L.M. Montgomery sat at the head. Her hair was piled up, which they did in those days. It was not a bun, but swept up and held in place with pins, as I recall. I believe Anita was beside me, between where I sat and where L.M. Montgomery was. I remember there didn't seem to be a lot of light in the house. The living room was dark, but the dining room was to the right and it was well lit. It must have been fall or early winter, because it was dark so early.

"I didn't get the impression that she was hearty or jovial. I felt she probably kept to herself very much. I guess her thoughts were off somewhere else. She was gracious, however. I wished I had the ability to carry on a scintillating conversation like Anne would have, but I couldn't do that, I was just too shy. I didn't even know what to call her. I knew I couldn't call her L.M. Montgomery, but somehow I couldn't bring myself to say 'Mrs. Macdonald' either.

"She was extremely friendly with me when I wore the dress at the pageant, and I felt very much at ease with her, but then, the night at her house, she was different. That's also what made me think that there was something going on that had nothing to do with me."

Olive wearing L.M. Montgomery's wedding dress in a church pageant, circa 1939.

Courtesy Reverend Linda Sparks.

"Green Gables," Cavendish, P.E.I.

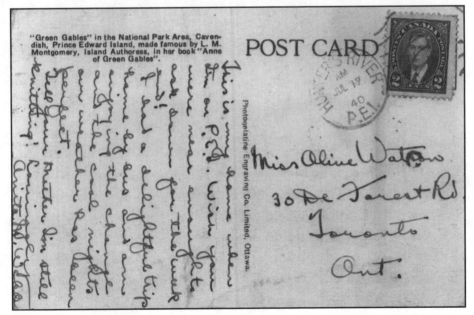

The postcard Anita sent to Olive from Green Gables (front and back views).

Courtesy Reverend Linda Sparks.

Betty Ball

A fan of L.M. Montgomery's, Betty Ball was living in the east end of Toronto when she decided to interview L.M. Montgomery for her school newspaper.

"When I was sixteen, I was a student at Malvern Collegiate and I had heard that L.M. Montgomery was living in Toronto. I was able to secure her address, and I wrote and asked if I could interview her for our school magazine. It was a long time before she replied, but she'd been out of town. The handwritten letter said: *I am sorry I could not answer your letter sooner, but I have been away from home a great deal. When I was home, I was so terribly busy trying to overtake some extra work that I could not arrange for the interview you asked for. I could give you a little time between Christmas and New Year's, if that would suit you. If not, after New Year's. Suppose you ring me up on the phone: Junction 9503 and we can choose a time to suit us both. Yours Cordially, L.M. Montgomery Macdonald.*

Maud in a field of daisies in Prince Edward Island.

Courtesy Prince Edward Island Public Archives and Records Office.

"I called and she arranged for me to come between Christmas and New Year's, 1936. She lived at 210A Riverside Drive. I was only sixteen and I didn't drive, so my parents drove me out. It was a lovely home. I walked into a central hall, and the living room was on the left. The staircase was either to the right or in front. It was a real entrance hall.

"I was extremely nervous; I didn't know what to ask. I liked the idea of interviewing her but I didn't know what to say. Every question I ever thought of asking her went right out of my head. She put me at ease right away and told me a few things and showed me Gog and Magog, the china dogs with gold spots that were standing one on each side of the fireplace. We visited in the living room. Everything seemed to be on the dark side. The living room wasn't bright, there were only soft lamps, and L.M. Montgomery was dressed in a dark afternoon dress.

"We just talked for a while. Her voice was quiet, well modulated. I did not see her husband at all, and she didn't refer to him either. I remarked about the movie star Anne Shirley who had played the part of Anne Shirley in the original *Anne of Green Gables* movie and then took that name as her movie name. And L.M. Montgomery said, *Oh yes, I still keep in touch with her. In fact, that bowl of fruit was sent to me from Anne Shirley this Christmas.* There was a bowl of huge California oranges and other fruit. Then one of her sons came in through the French doors in the living room and said, *I'm going out for a little while, I won't be long.* He was quite nice, the way he spoke to her. She said, *Alright, then, you won't be late.* And he said, *No.* I remember that because I thought he was a man and it struck me as odd that he was living at home still. He was dark and fairly well built, not thin at all.

"I think she had just been to Prince Edward Island and [that] they were just beginning to talk about starting things [such as museums] to recognize her down there. She told me that she didn't write the Anne stories in chronological order, and I remember putting that in my article. She was so charming, so very nice, and looked a lot like the last pictures I remember of her."

Mary Skinner

Mary's father, Reverend Alexander Ross Skinner, was the minister at Avenue Road Presbyterian Church in Toronto, and her mother was acquainted with L.M. Montgomery through the Presbyterian Ministers' Wives Association. L.M. Montgomery graciously agreed to come to the Skinners' church and speak in order to help raise funds for the church.

"I guess I was a bit past high school, it was probably 1940 or '41 — or maybe a little before. My mother was a member of the Ministers' Wives Association for the Presbyterian churches in Toronto, and she was on a committee that lined up entertainers or speakers to come to the church and, for a small fee, would help us to raise money. Evidently, my mother must have met Mrs. Macdonald at a meeting of the Ministers' Wives. Mrs. Macdonald very kindly agreed to come one evening and give a lecture at our church, Avenue Road Presbyterian. I invited a couple of my high school friends, who of course were also interested in hearing L.M. Montgomery speak. I'd won some sort of award when I was much younger, and as a prize I'd been given *Emily of New Moon*. So that was the first L.M. Montgomery book I read. I don't remember getting around to the Anne books until a bit later.

"Mrs. Macdonald gave an excellent lecture. It was about some of the problems you ran into when you were imagining characters and then placing them in a specific spot. And whether you changed the name — you would think of some town or village or whatever, but you would need to change the name of the place. And then you would imagine your story. She had written a book and in it she had written about a family she called the proud Lesleys. Now, the name came out of her imagination. It was not, as far as she knew, applicable to anybody. I mean, there weren't any Lesleys in the area. However, she told us that she got protests from various people because there did happen to be, in a town with the very same name she'd given the town in the book, a very proud family who were really stuck up and sort of lorded it over their neighbours. So she had quite a time about that. I found the lecture fascinating.

"My sister Muriel also attended the talk and we discussed what L.M. Montgomery was wearing that evening. We both think she was wearing something dark. I thought it was blue, Muriel thought it was brown. But we're both a little uncertain. She did have a hat. My memory of her is very much like the pictures of her in some of the journal books. I remember her as being short to average height. She reminded me quite a bit of my mother, who was little as well. Afterwards we served tea and coffee and cookies. When entertainers came, it was the minister's family who supplied the refreshments. L.M. Montgomery talked to people at the reception; she got absorbed in talking to a few people. Since I already had the book *Emily of New Moon*, my mother suggested that maybe Mrs. Macdonald would autograph it for me, so I went up and got my copy and brought it down and she did give me an autograph with the little cat signature. I loved the Anne books, too, but I preferred the Emily books. I told Mrs. Macdonald that, and it was my impression that she was pleased to hear that. She was sort of thin, as far as I can remember. Her voice was clear. She spoke very well and very clearly. I was totally taken by the lecture. I thought it was very interesting."

Desmond Newell

Desmond Newell worked for L.M. Montgomery's publishers, McClelland and Stewart. As one of their top-selling authors, Maud had an open invitation to drop by the publishing company to pick up new books.

"I was a representative with McClelland and Stewart. Mrs. Montgomery [Macdonald] would come in about once every two or three months. And if I was there, Mr. McClelland always got me to look after her. I have a kind countenance [laughs]. We got on very well and she used to tease me about Ireland — I hadn't been in Canada for very long. I guess I have an accent. She'd say, *Oh, I like the way you said that*, or something like that. Just quietly. She was an avid reader and so was I. She was very ladylike, quiet. She reminded me of my Sunday school teacher years and years ago and she had a quiet sense of humour and we'd sit down and talk. I was allowed to give her up to twelve books. She was an avid reader of detective stories.

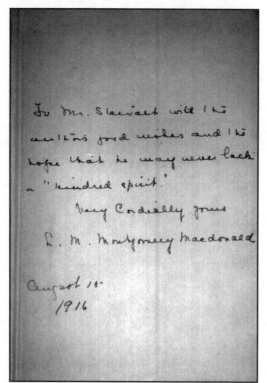

A signed inscription to Maud's publisher, Mr. Stewart of McClelland and Stewart, 1916.

"I picked them out for her and I'd bring them down in two parcels. She usually had a taxi or a friend waiting. She'd read them and then come back in another three months or so. And each time she got approximately twelve books. She was a thin, frail-looking woman. I knew fairly well what she wanted because I read the books myself and we'd talk over the ones I'd given her, so I got to know better each time what sort of books she would like and I'd try to pick out what would please her. She liked mostly detective books: Doubleday series; Scribner's had some; some

One of the last known photos of L.M. Montgomery, taken at a cottage in Grimsby. Maud is standing in the centre with a light-coloured coat, and Ewan is standing, second from left.

Courtesy John Wallace and Judy Koshan.

of the English mysteries; and also from the American publishers Morrow. She liked those ones. She was ill the last time she came, and because she wasn't well, she just stayed a short time. Shortly after that, she died. She was a very charming lady, and we sold a lot of her books all over the country. I was very fond of her. She was very, very nice. But at times, you know, I thought she seemed a little sad when discussing things. She spoke a bit of the Island and I said to her, *Yes, I must go when I get a chance.* I did go to Prince Edward Island and I saw where she grew up. I was very sorry to hear when she died."

Chapter Six
Articles about L.M. Montgomery, 1909–1942

This chapter contains articles on and interviews with L.M. Montgomery. Only one was published posthumously, written very shortly after her death by Ephraim Weber, one of her long-time pen-pals. Maud had exchanged letters with Mr. Weber even before *Anne of Green Gables* had made her famous. They also met, but their friendship was conducted for the most part through the written word, and his article gives us another intimate look at one aspect of her life.

The articles and interviews show how L.M. Montgomery was perceived by the press and the public while she was living. They give insights into her upbringing; her writing techniques; and her life as a minister's wife and a mother.

Both Canadian and American spellings of various words remain as they were in the original articles. Several factual errors are numbered and clarified.

Miss Montgomery, the Author of the "Anne"

A Short Pen Sketch of the Young Prince Edward Island Authoress, who has Achieved Distinction as the Creator of a Delightful Character in Fiction.

By A. Wylie Mahon

(*Canadian Bookman*, November 1909)

Few names in Canadian literature are so well known to-day as that of Miss L.M. Montgomery, "Lucy Maud," as the proud Prince Edward Islanders love to call her. It may be partly owing to their insular position — although no one would care to advance this theory too openly whilst sojourning amongst the thrifty, sharp-witted, and delightfully hospitable people of that beautiful little province — that the Islanders are so clannish. The people as a whole feel that they have a provincial, proprietary right, almost a family interest in those of their number who are distinguishing themselves in the world of life or literature. President J.G. Schurman, of Cornell, will always be "Jacob" to many of them; and Professor D.J. Fraser, of Montreal, will always be "Dan." The more charming and popular books Miss Montgomery writes the more tenaciously will the proud Prince Edward Islanders hold on to "Lucy Maud."

Miss Montgomery's home is at Cavendish, on the north side of the Island, where she can look out upon the broad Gulf of St. Lawrence, and dream dreams and see visions, and exercise her imagination unrestrainedly, no Rachel Lynde daring to make her afraid, although it is hinted that Rachel's original does live and move and have her being in that charming countryside.

Miss Montgomery belongs to an exceptionally clever, brainy family. The Rev. L.G. Macneill, the pastor-emeritus of St. Andrew's Church, St. John, N.B., who is recognized as one of the ablest preachers Canada has produced, is her uncle. Mr. Chester Macneill, so well known on the Pacific coast, is also her uncle; and Professor Macneill of Dalhousie College, Halifax, is her cousin.

Miss Montgomery showed the bent of her genius for story telling almost as early in life as Sir Walter Scott himself. When a mere child she began to write stories in which her cats, with their comical names, appeared as the principal characters. Whatever else the cats lacked, they did not lack imagination. They could imagine very much after the manner of Anne Shirley herself.

It would be interesting to-day to read those first attempts at literature on the part of this popular writer, if some one had preserved them as the mother of Charles Kingsley in her place of concealment took down her child's sermons which he preached to the chairs in the nursery.

At a very early age Miss Montgomery began contributing stories and bits of verse to the local papers, some of which attracted a good deal of attention in her Island province. The writer knows one person who came across some verses written by her when she was not very far advanced in her teens which impressed him so favorably that he ventured to prophesy that the larger world would some day know the name of Lucy Maud Montgomery. This man rests his reputation as a literary prophet upon this prediction which is being very rapidly fulfilled these days when "Anne of Green Gables," and the younger Anne of literature that is the older Anne of life, "Anne of Avonlea," are amongst the best sellers, and will soon require six figures to represent the number sold.

Miss Montgomery is a prodigious worker, as any one might readily infer from a hasty glance over the popular magazines and periodicals of the day where her name is so frequently to be found. She is now engaged on a new book which her friends believe will rival in interest and popularity the "Anne" books.

A few months ago in a review of the Canadian literature of the Atlantic provinces a writer in one of our weekly journals made some reference to Miss Montgomery. When this appeared in print the "Miss" had been converted into a "Mrs." The writer immediately wrote Miss Montgomery and assured her that he was not to blame for making a "Mrs." of her. He told her that being a clergyman, and properly registered in the province in which he resided, he was legally qualified to make a "Mrs." of her, if she were to appear before him with all the necessary documents, and also a man; but under existing circumstances, the woman and the man and the documents all being absent, he had no power to make a "Mrs." of her.

Miss Montgomery wrote an exceedingly clever and characteristic reply to this letter, assuring the clergyman that far worse things than that had happened to her in print. Some had made a "Mr." of her. That was hard to bear. She said that she had no unovercomable repugnance, such as some mythical females of uncertain age were supposed to have, to the term "Mrs." This, of course, presupposed a kindred spirit. Rachel Lynde, who is an authority in all such matters, whispers that there is a kindred spirit in Miss Montgomery's world, in the realm of divinity. But I must not repeat what Rachel says.

L.M. Montgomery

The creator of "Anne of Green Gables" as she appears to those who know her in her home-life as Mrs. Ewan Macdonald, a charming wife and mother as well as the writer of numerous delightful books.

By Marjorie MacMurchy[1]

(*The Island Patriot*, November 1, 1913)

The Golden Road, the latest of L.M. Montgomery's books, was her sixth book of fiction. By this time we may sum up clearly the qualities of a writer in whose life one of the most influential facts is that she was born in Prince Edward Island. The world that reads her books — for her books are immensely popular, the sales amounting to half a million copies — is a world of good people, everyday and workaday people who are happy to warm their hearts in the good-will, sunshine, and promise-of-good-coming-true which are a great part of the gift of this woman story-writer of Prince Edward Island. We read her stories eagerly because they are true and happy and full of a clear, kind, wholesome, northern simplicity. One wonders if other people find in Miss Montgomery's work a certain likeness to the writings of Hans Christian Andersen. He is a northern writer, clear, simple and truth-telling. Miss Montgomery's creative power is less, but in saying so one detracts nothing from the value of her work as it stands. Hans Christian Andersen is a world writer. It is true that by instinct Miss Montgomery is not so economical of words as Hans Andersen was. Her *Chronicles of Avonlea* had less of the flowery diction which sometimes threatens her simplicity; but *The Golden Road* has more of it. Pretty strings of words and fanciful names are not to be compared in value with her plain straightforward happy telling of a happy story. Her knowledge of northern character is worth its weight in gold; and economy in words is much to ask from anyone, since it is one of the final proofs of greatness in a writer.

To trace the connection between Miss Montgomery's gift as a story-writer and Prince Edward Island is a delightful task. If the fairies live anywhere in Canada it must be in Prince Edward Island, with its red earth, gentle aspects, loveliness of fields and broken belts of wood in darker green, and the blue sea coming up on every side. The people are shrewd, kind, self-respecting, full of character and thrift, fond of themselves, their Island and their traditions with a certain degree of passion, and very much disposed to play.

> "She said to me to take life easy
> As the grass grows in the field."

That is Prince Edward Island. It is a dear place.

But more to our present purpose, which is tracing the true descent and inheritance of a story-writer, the Island is crammed with stories, stories of sailors and great storms, stories of ghosts and the Devil, stories of lovers and wooing and runaway matches, stories of queer people and witches, stories of the good little people themselves. Even I have seen the silver rim of a water pitcher that was broken one night on the way to the well — but that *is* another story.

Miss Montgomery was born in Prince Edward Island sometime in the seventies or eighties of the nineteenth century. Her mother died when she was very young. Her father went soon to Saskatchewan. The child was given to the care of her mother's father and mother. Her maternal grandfather was postmaster at Cavendish, a circumstance which later was to mean a great deal to the young story-writer. Every budding genius requires reams of blank paper. The yellowy-brown post-office forms of the Dominion Government were trove to her. She scribbled on their yellow backs to her heart's content. Thus do governments encourage unaware the genius of young citizens. Later when manuscripts were sent out to editors, Miss Montgomery is herself authority for the statement that being able to recover the rejected mss. from the post office without a soul except herself being the wiser made all the difference in the world. She would never have had the courage to keep on sending if the post office had been elsewhere.

Her maternal grandfather's name was Macneill. The Macneills are famous Island people. Also be it recorded, a Scottish poet named Macneill was one of Miss Montgomery's ancestors. He wrote at least three lovely songs which have survived in Scottish poetry, "Saw ye my wee thing, saw ye my ain thing?" "Come under my Pladie," often wrongly attributed to Burns, and "I lo'ed n'er a laddie but aue." These romantic countryside gleams of genius, of passion, tenderness and fidelity which make Scottish love songs so poignant and exquisite came fitfully to Canada in emigrant ships. Such a tradition came with the Macneills. There were two brothers Macneill, Miss Montgomery's great uncles, both of whom were poets on the Island. They were noted for their gift of celebrating local happenings in satirical verse. It was then the fashion in Prince Edward Island to take off the foibles of one's neighbours and the incidents of local history in rhyming couplets. These were not committed to paper, but were recited at evening gatherings. When one of these clever gentlemen, the Macneills, was occupied with the work of the farm his mind would be busy putting into rhyme the exploits of neighbor Angus or neighbor Neil, the election of the local member of Parliament, the courting of Nancy or the runaway match of Peter and Bessie. At that time boiling potatoes — a famous Island product — for equally famous Island porkers took up hours of time and afforded mental leisure for the poetical efforts of the Island satirist. It was in this incomparable school for a story-writer that the little girl heard Island stories and learned to understand northern character. By and by when grandfather Macneill died, her grandmother continued in the Government appointment as postmistress. All the neighbors were cousins or cousins' cousins, uncles and aunts, and the incidents of daily life in the neighborhood came flying into the post office as a flock of hens will to the center of a barnyard at the call of the mistress when it is time to scatter provender. But before this Miss Montgomery had been at Dalhousie College for a year. Again, in another year she did some writing for the Halifax "Chronicle." But at the end of a year Miss Montgomery had to give up her work in the

"Chronicle" office and return to the Island. Her grandmother Macneill was growing old and needed her. From this time on her grandmother could not bear to have her away from the house scarcely for a day. Then out of years of writing stories came the wonderful success of *Anne of Green Gables*. The Island lady of stories who lived at Cavendish in a few months had friends by the hundred who lived all over North America. As she said once, "I think every red-haired girl in the world must have written to me." These friendships have meant a great deal to Miss Montgomery. Once before her grandmother's death she visited her publisher, Mr. L.C. Page, in Boston. *Anne of Green Gables* was followed by *Anne of Avonlea*, and *Kilmeny*. In the summer of 1911, following her grandmother's death, Miss Montgomery married the Rev. Ewan Macdonald, who is the minister of the Presbyterian church in Leaskdale, Ontario. Since then she has published *The Story Girl*, *The Chronicles of Avonlea*, and now *The Golden Road*, a sequel to *The Story Girl*. Her gift is too ardent and compelling not to force for itself an outlet in stories. Story writing is as natural to her as living. Her little son, born on the first Sunday in July, 1912, has made life full to the uttermost. Leaskdale is a quaint home-like Ontario village seven miles from a railway station. The neighborhood, like most Ontario neighborhoods, is an excellent field for study of Canadian and Scottish character. But there is not a sign that Miss Montgomery has exhausted her Island studies. She may never even have thought of writing an Ontario story.

So far only one side of Miss Montgomery's ancestry has been mentioned. The Montgomerys of the Island are equally famous with the Macneills. Miss Montgomery's father's father was Senator Montgomery who lived to a great age and long represented the Island at Ottawa. There is a story that the Montgomery family came to live in Prince Edward Island by the determination of a woman. On a certain ship from Scotland came a Montgomery and his wife and family. The voyage was long and stormy and finally the ship's supply of drinking water was almost at an end. Mrs. Montgomery had been constantly seasick for more than six weeks. The captain pitying her when he sent his sailors ashore to the Island which was the nearest land, said she might go with them. The lady accepted the captain's offer. But when the sailors were ready to return to the ship she declared that nothing would induce her to set foot on shipboard again. Expostulation was in vain. Mrs. Montgomery remained firm and as a matter of necessity her husband and children had to be landed on Prince Edward Island. There are descendants of this lady living in most of the nine Canadian provinces to-day. Miss L.M. Montgomery is one of them. The true benefit and blessing which comes to those who read Miss Montgomery's stories is in her delineation of a sane, wholesome and delightful social fabric. Here are standards which have not been confused or broken. Fever and strife do not exist in these stories. Stalwart character, strength of will, intellectual and moral soundness, goodwill, gayety, common sense and happiness are rated simply as the best thing in life. There is no preaching. Money is a servant, not a master. Luxury is never mentioned. The foundation of the northern character which Miss Montgomery shows us is well and truly laid. Laughter and happiness and health are accompaniment of good life which is normal life. Something like this is the interpretation of Miss Montgomery's work as a story-writer which is at the same time an interpretation of Prince Edward Island. No wonder that the hearts of Islanders in their dreams turn home.

"Anne of Green Gables" is Story of Miss L.M. Montgomery's Childhood

She Is Now Mrs. Ewan Macdonald and No Longer
Lives in Prince Edward Island

MADE KNOWN BY HER

To the Wide World — A Natural Story-Teller —
Treasures in the Leaskdale Manse.

By Marjorie MacMurchy

(*The Toronto Star Weekly*, April 18, 1914)

The author of "Anne of Green Gables" still signs her stories "L.M. Montgomery" although in 1911 she married the Rev. Ewan Macdonald, of Leaskdale, Ontario, who at one time had been the Presbyterian minister at the settlement of Cavendish in Prince Edward Island, where he met the writer who was afterwards to become one of the most popular of present-day authors.

No Canadian Province has any more passionately devoted citizen than Mrs. Montgomery Macdonald is of Prince Edward Island. She was born at Clifton, P.E.I., in 1877.[2] Her mother died soon after her birth, and she was taken to live with her maternal grandparents at Cavendish. Her grandfather, Mr. MacNeill,[3] was postmaster of the settlement. As soon as she was able to run about, her play-mates were cousins and the children of neighbors. Everyone knows who has read Miss Montgomery's stories how common it is in Prince Edward Island for neighborhoods to be closely related. To this day, with the most vivid distinctness, the author will describe every nook and cranny, every pasture field and slope of her island home. There was one sloping field where every spring they went to look for wild flowers. A day came when the field was ploughed, and the little girl thought her heart would break. Near the homestead, she remembers, was their playhouse. Its walls were built only in imagination. But the children had fastened a door to a tree, and everyone who came into the playhouse had to come by the door. It is this vivid remembrance of the scenes of her childhood, and her passionate attachment to every inch of ground and every memory, which is part of Miss Montgomery's gift as a story writer. Like Robert Louis Stevenson, Miss Montgomery has never wholly lost the spirit of childhood. In her heart she is still the girl who played in Prince Edward Island.

Stayed West But a Year

When she was a child of twelve or so her father sent for her to join him in Saskatchewan.[4] He had married a second time, and his daughter, Lucy Maud, had several step-brothers and step-sisters.[5] But the little Island girl stayed only a year in the West. She was lonely for her home by the sea. The schools of the island are good schools. After leaving the Cavendish school, L.M. Montgomery attended Prince of Wales College in Charlottetown. Later she spent a year at Dalhousie University in Halifax. While she was in Halifax she did some work for one of the Halifax papers.[6] Her university course had to be given up since after the death of her grandfather her Grandmother MacNeill needed her at home.[7]

When her husband died Mrs. MacNeill was appointed postmistress. Miss Montgomery has often said that she would never have had the courage to send out her stories if the post-office had been in a neighbor's house. She could send away manuscripts and get them back again without a soul in Cavendish but herself being any the wiser. When she was a little girl she used to write many stories, and the paper she used was the back of the Government forms sent to the post-office. Anyone who has read "Anne of Green Gables," and "Anne of

Avonlea," knows exactly how joyous and delightful Miss Montgomery's girl-hood was: it is faithfully described in these stories.

"Anne of Green Gables" had been to a good many publishers before Mr. L.C. Page of Boston perceived what a charming creation the little girl was. Mark Twain spoke of Anne as the "sweetest creation of child life" yet written. The Canadian poet Bliss Carman called her one of the immortal children of fiction. The author found that she had made friends all over the world. "Anne of Green Gables" had not been her first story. She had published several seri-als, mostly in Sunday School publications.[8] But when "Anne of Green Gables" charmed the reading public, Miss Montgomery had some stories on hand which she could dispose of at once without the least difficulty.[9]

Her Later Books

Her later books have been: "Anne of Avonlea" (1909); "Kilmeny of the Orchard" (1910); "The Story Girl" (1911); "Chronicles of Avonlea" (1912); "The Golden Road," a sequel to "The Story Girl," was published in 1913. All these books, with the exception of "The Chronicles of Avonlea," have been stories of a radiant childhood in Prince Edward Island. "The Chronicles" is a collection of short stories, mainly of grown-up people. These have splendid humor and give an admirable analysis of Island character. They somewhat resemble Miss Jewett's beautiful stories of New England, and they are consid-ered as being probably Miss Montgomery's best work, although scarcely as pop-ular as the delightful Anne stories. Miss Montgomery has written as well a con-siderable amount of descriptive verse, much of which has appeared in Canadian and American magazines. A few years ago the Christmas number of *Harper's Magazine* contained one of Miss Montgomery's poems.

The Manse at Leaskdale has many Island treasures. Leaskdale is seven miles from a railway station. It is a little cluster of houses in a typical country neigh-borhood of Ontario. The little son of the Manse has been once down to the sea. "Punchkins" is a beautiful baby. There is a remarkable cat which traveled up from Prince Edward Island in a crate when his mistress came to Ontario.[10] He is apparently quite reconciled to his new home. On a table in the drawing-room stands a jug about which clings typical Island memories. The story of this jug explains in some measure one of the reasons why Miss Montgomery is a maker of stories. All the winds of the world have blown many stories to Prince Edward Island. It is not to be wondered at that a Prince Edward Island woman has been gifted with the genius of a story-teller. Indeed, the MacNeills brought the writing gift over from Scotland with them. The Scottish song-writer who wrote "Saw ye my wee thing, saw ye my ain thing?" and "Come under my Plaidie" belonged to the same family of Montgomerys.

The Jug's Story

But here is the story of the jug.[11] There was a sailor once whose love lived in Scotland, and he had this jug made for her in a foreign country. He had her name painted on the jug in the centre of a nosegay of painted flowers. But on the voyage he was drowned, and when the ship came into port, the captain gave the jug to the sailor's sweetheart. Years afterwards, when she died, she gave it to her sister who came out from Scotland to Prince Edward Island, and on the voyage across it was usefully filled with black currant jam. The jug was in the dairy filled with cream when Miss Montgomery begged for it. The sailor's sweetheart's sister was the story-writer's grandmother.

Prince Edward Island chronicles are crowded with stories like this and it was in such an atmosphere that the gift of this writer was fostered. The red earth of the Island, the green fields, the blue sea water, are a setting for many romantic stories, many a curious chronicle of human nature. It is a lovely country, with a lyrical softness in its beauty. But there have been shipwrecks on the shores. Miss Montgomery says she remembers a shipwrecked crew of foreigners who spent one summer near her grandfather's place. They used to drive about the Island in a wagon, shouting as they drove past, exactly as if they had been pirates out of a story by Stevenson. The Island people have been wise. They lead happy lives, with many social enjoyments and recreations: they do not work too hard; they value highly what is most valuable in life. This is the life which Miss Montgomery has painted so joyously for the world. The latest Island romance is the romance of the fox-ranches; but whether or not Mrs. Montgomery Macdonald will write of this, time will show. She had only now come, one would judge, into full possession of her powers as a writer of stories.

(Reprinted with permission — The Toronto Star Syndicate.)

The Author of Anne

By Ethel Chapman

(*Maclean's*, October 1919)

There is one heroine of Canadian fiction who will never be criticized as exotic or lacking in inspiration — the winsome, gingery, red-headed girl who grew up through "Anne of Green Gables," "Anne of Avonlea," "Anne of the Island" and blossomed into full womanhood two years ago in "Anne's House of Dreams." As an ideal for the young womanhood of the country she has a place all her own, this girl of imagination and wit and dreams, strangely combined with practical common sense, to whom the blossoming cherry tree outside her window was a "Snow Queen" and the pond across the flats "The Lake of Shining Waters," who found in the woods of silver birches a realm of "kindred spirits" and who could keep house and teach school and help most efficiently in the bringing up of two very human waifs of children. No wonder mothers want their daughters to read the Anne books.

From the first appearance of "Anne of Green Gables" the books "caught on." This winter Anne is going to appear in the movies. The scenario rights to the four books, "Anne of Green Gables," "Anne of Avonlea," "Chronicles of Avonlea" and "Anne of the Island" have been bought by the Famous Players — Lasky Corporation. A Canadian movie with the quaint and beautiful setting of the farms and orchards of Prince Edward Island, written by a Canadian author! We have been waiting for this for a long time. But the author herself, now the wife of Rev. Macdonald, the Presbyterian minister at Leaskdale and the mother of two sturdy, quick-brained boys, doesn't seem to consider it an event of more importance than the next church christening.

It has been said that in the first two Anne books, Miss Montgomery drew from the experiences of her own life. Certainly Anne got her imagination from no one else, but it is not the author's own story. "My places are real places," she says, "but my people are imaginary." They have certain points in common, however. Miss Montgomery's mother died before she was two years old and she went to live with her grandmother, which no doubt gave her her sympathetic understanding of Anne's little problems in a home with only elderly people. What she lacked in the way of companionship with other children, however, seems to have been more than made up by a natural environment uniquely fitted to inspire the imagination. Her home was on a farm near Cavendish on the north shore of the Island and she says, "Tourists who travel by train through the Island have no idea of the beauty of its scenery because they do not see the north shore." She has in her home several striking pictures of the rocks and beaches along this coast, one of particular interest being a painting of the sand dunes along a favorite bathing beach — one of the finest bathing beaches in the world, by the way — where the winds had cupped out a hollow that, as children, they used for a dressing-room.

It is not surprising that she loves the sea. "When I was a child," she says, "I practically lived at the shore during the mackerel fishing season. My grandfather, like all the other farmers around, had a fishing boat, and from the time the mackerel came in till the end of the season, the men would get up at four o'clock in the morning and go down to the sea. At seven o'clock we children would take their breakfast to them. If the fishing was particularly good they would sometimes stay all day and we would bring all their meals and spend the intervals between wading in the surf and climbing over the rocks ... I get homesick for the sea sometimes yet."

Yet with all her fondness for the outdoors we gather that little Maud must have been "a dark and eerie child," wandering off by herself to commune with imaginary people or revelling in whatever books were available and already creating her own little stories. "I can imagine," she says, "what it would be to be a drunkard for reading. Fortunately my English grandmother saw to it that I did the practical things as well. There were no lending libraries on the Island at that time and our library at home was a rather unusual collection to satisfy the reading tastes of a child. We had full sets of Dickens, Scott and all the poets;

Pilgrim's Progress and *Paradise Lost*, which I was allowed to read on Sundays; E.P. Roe's stories, admitted because of their religious setting, and the Pansy books. Personally I was fond of boys' books, adventure and anything dramatic. I don't think I would have liked the kind of books I write."

But neither her early reading nor her picturesque surroundings can be wholly responsible for her literary gifts. Dreamers and writers are born as well as made, and it is not surprising that she is a direct descendant of one of the lesser Scottish poets, the Hector MacNeill who wrote "Come Under My Plaidie," "Saw Ye My Wee Thing, Saw Ye My Ain Thing?" and "I Lo'e Ne'er a Laddie But One." She also had a grand-uncle — one of the undiscovered poets who composed verse which those who remember it appreciate now as real poetry. Unfortunately he never put his compositions on paper. He created them as he worked about his little Prince Edward Island farm, and at night recited them to the children while they sat around a sugar kettle hung over a fire in the yard where he boiled potatoes for his pigs.

When she grew up, Miss Montgomery taught school for three years. She was already writing stories and this was probably when she did her hardest work, getting up at five o'clock in the morning and writing till seven. "And on winter mornings before the fire had warmed the farm house through, it was some chore," she admits. Later she spent one winter at newspaper work in Halifax, but at the death of her grandfather she went home to be with her grandmother. Perhaps this was a fortunate thing as it led her to give all her time to story writing.

"The first story I was ever paid for," she says, "was published in 'Golden Days,' a Philadelphia magazine which has since gone under. I don't know whether my stories killed it or not. They gave me five dollars and I have never been so rich in my life. I had had stories published before this and had received subscriptions to the magazines. It was while I was making my living writing short stories that I sneaked time to do 'Anne of Green Gables' just to please myself. I believe that was the reason for its spontaneity. Five times I sent it out and five times it was returned. The last publisher wrote: 'Our reader has found some merit in it but not enough to warrant publication.' This 'damning with faint praise' was the last straw. I put the story away and left it for a while. One day at housecleaning time I brought it out again and looked it over. As girl's stuff, I thought, that's not too bad, and I tried again. I had an alphabetical list of publishers, had tried everything that seemed possible down to the P's, so I sent it to Page and it was accepted."

"Kilmeny of the Orchard" had been written before this and published as a serial in the *American Housekeeper,* another defunct magazine. When it appeared in book form one critic wrote that it was obviously a product of the pride of authorship hurriedly gotten out to sell on the merits of the other.

Two years later "Anne of Avonlea" was published. It was about this time that Miss Montgomery was married to the Rev. Macdonald, and came to the manse at Leaskdale. Mr. Macdonald had formerly been the minister in her home church at Cavendish. "Chronicles of Avonlea" had been written before her marriage but was not published until after. Since coming to Ontario she has written "The Golden Road," "Anne of the Island," "Anne's House of Dreams," and her latest book "Rainbow Valley" went on the book stands in August.

"I think I'll always write of the Island," she says. And one only needs to hear her talk of the Island and to see the relics from the Island that she treasures in her Ontario home, to know that her first love has left a lasting impression. She has paintings of "The Lake of Shining Waters" and "The Lover's Lane," which figures especially in "Anne of Avonlea," and which was really the place where the author used to wander out in the evenings to "think out" her stories ready for writing the next morning.

But we prophesy that some day Mrs. Macdonald will write a shore story with an individuality and color quite as appealing as that of the Anne books. She has a wealth of legend and story of the coast life, for the quiet little island has had its sea tragedies as well as its romances by land. There was "the great American storm of 1851," and she says, "If you have ever seen a storm in the Gulf you'll never forget it. It has a bite and a tang that no land storm could possibly have. At this time American fishing vessels used to come into the gulf for mackerel. This particular storm drove hundreds of these vessels onto the north coast, and for weeks afterwards the men of the Island gathered the bodies from the shore and buried them in the Cavendish churchyard. Many of the graves are there to this day, nameless and unknown."

The author of Anne does not devote herself entirely to the making of books. She is a woman of personal charm and winsomeness, as broad-minded and practical as she is imaginative, with a keen sense of humor, happy in the keeping of her home and the interests of the parish. She is a mother who mothers her children personally; they have always been considered before her books. When she has efficient help in the house she locks herself in her room and writes for two hours every morning; at other times she does her own house-keeping with the skill and dispatch of a woman trained to it. She even takes her knitting with her on her pastoral visits; it was soldiers' socks during the war, and since then she has nearly completed a bed spread of the kind you expect to find on some old mahogany, lavender-scented spare bed-room. She is just about what you would expect the author of Anne to be.

Fiction Writers on Fiction Writing, 1923

One hundred and sixteen successful authors were sent questionnaires about their writing habits and careers. Their answers were published in the book *Fiction Writers on Fiction Writing*, edited by Arthur Sullivant Hoffman and published in 1923 by the Bobbs-Merrill Company, Indianapolis. The following excerpt presents only a portion of the book, the questionnaire as answered by L.M. Montgomery.

What is the genesis of a story with you — does it grow from an incident, a character, a trait of character, a situation, setting, a title, or what? That is, what do you mean by an idea for a story?

L.M. Montgomery: The genesis of my stories is very varied. Sometimes the character suggests the story. For instance, in my first book, *Anne of Green Gables*, the whole story was modeled around the character of "Anne" and arranged to suit her. Most of my books are similar in origin. The characters seem to grow in my mind, much after the oft-quoted "Topsy" manner, and when they are fully incubated I arrange a setting for them, choosing incidents and surroundings which will harmonize with and develop them. With short stories it is different. There I generally start with an idea — some incident which I elaborate and invent characters to suit, thus reversing the process I employ in book-writing. A very small germ will sometimes blossom out quite amazingly. One of my most successful short stories owed its origin to the fact that one day I heard a lady — a refined person usually of irreproachable language — use a point-blank "cuss-word" in a moment of great provocation. Again, the fact that I heard of a man forbidding his son to play the violin because he thought it was wicked furnished the idea for the best short story I ever wrote.

Do you map it out in advance, or do you start with, say, a character or situation, and let the story tell itself as you write? Do you write it in pieces to be joined together, or straightaway as a whole? Is the ending clearly in mind when you begin? To what extent do you revise?

L.M. Montgomery: I map everything out in advance. When I have developed plot, characters and incidents in my mind I write out a "skeleton" of the story or book. In the case of a book, I divide it into so many "sections" — usually eight or nine — representing the outstanding periods in the story. In each section I write down what characters are necessary, what they do, what their setting is, and quite a bit of what they say. When the skeleton is complete I begin the actual writing, and so thoroughly have I become saturated with the story during the making of the skeleton that I feel as if I were merely describing and setting down something that I have actually seen happening, and the clothing of the dry bones with flesh goes on rapidly and easily. This does not, however, prevent changes taking place as I write. Sometimes an incident I had thought was going to be very minor assumes major proportions or *vice versa*. Sometimes, too, characters grow or dwindle contrary to my first intentions. But on the whole I follow my plan pretty closely and the ending is very often written out quite fully in the last "section" before a single word of the first chapter is written. I revise very extensively and the "notes" with which my completed manuscript is peppered are surely and swiftly bringing down my typist's gray hairs with sorrow to the grave. But these revisions deal only with descriptions and conversation. Characters, plots and incidents are never changed.

When you read a story to what extent does your imagination reproduce the story-world of another author — do you actually see in your imagination all the characters, action and setting just as if you were looking at an actual scene? Do you actually hear all sounds described, mentioned and inferred, just as if they were real sounds? How real does your imagination make the smells in a story you read? Does your imagination make you feel actual physical pain corresponding, though in a slighter degree, to pain represented in a story?

L.M. Montgomery: Yes, when I read a story I *see* everything, exactly as if I were looking at an actual scene. I *hear* the sounds and *smell* the odors. When I read *Pickwick Papers* I have to make many an extra sneak to the pantry, so hungry do I become through reading of the bacon and eggs and milk punch in which the characters so frequently revel. I never feel *physical* pain when I read a story, no matter how intense the suffering described may be. But I feel *mental* pain so keenly that sometimes I can hardly bear to continue reading. Yet I do not dislike this sensation. On the contrary I like it. If I can have a jolly good howl several times in a book I am its friend for life. Yet, in every-day existence, I am the reverse of a tearful or sentimental person. No book do I love as I love *David Copperfield*. Yet during my many re-readings I must have wept literal quarts over David's boyish tribulations. And ghost stories that make me grow actually cold with fear are such as my soul loveth.

If you can really "see things with your eyes shut," what limitations?

L.M. Montgomery: "I can see things," with eyes shut or open, colors and all. Sometimes I see them mentally — that is, I realize that they are produced subjectively and are under the control of my will. But very often, when imagination has been specially stimulated, I seem really to see them objectively. In this case, however, I never see landscapes or anything but *faces* — and generally grotesque or comical faces. I never see a beautiful face. They crowd on my sight in a mob, flashing up for a second, then instantly filled by others. I always enjoy this "seeing things" immensely, but I can not do it at will.

If you studied solid geometry, did it give you more trouble than other mathematics?

L.M. Montgomery: The very name of geometry was a nightmare to me. I decline to discuss the horrible subject at all. Yet I loved algebra and had a mild affection for arithmetic. These things are predestinated.

Do you have stock pictures for, say, a village church or a cowboy, or does each case produce its individual vision?

L.M. Montgomery: I have no "stock pictures" as a reader. I generally see things pretty much as the writer describes them — though certainly not as the "movie" people seem to see them! This is especially true of places and things. But very few writers have the power to make me visualize their characters, even where they describe them minutely. Illustrations generally make matters worse. I detest illustrations in a story. It is only when there is some peculiarly striking and restrained bit of description attached to a character that I can *see* it. For example: When R.L. Stevenson in *Dr. Jekyll* says that there was something incredibly evil about "Hyde" — I am not quoting his exact words — I can see "Hyde" as clearly as I ever saw anything in my life. As a rule, I think the ability to describe characters so that readers may see them as clearly as they see their settings is a very rare gift among writers.

Is your response limited to the exact degree to which the author describes and makes vivid, or will the mere concept set you to reproducing just as vividly?

L.M. Montgomery: Yes, as a reader I *do* resent having too many images formed for me. I don't want too much description of anything or too many details in any description.

Is there any difference in behavior of your imagination when you are reading stories and when writing them?

L.M. Montgomery: When I *read* a story, I *see* people doing things in a certain setting; when I *write* a story I *am* the people myself and *live* their experiences.

When you write do you center your mind on the story itself or do you constantly have your readers in mind? In revising?

L.M. Montgomery: In writing a story I do not think of all these things — at least consciously. I never think of my readers at all. I think of myself. Does this story I am writing interest *me* as I write it — does it satisfy *me*? If so, there are enough people in the world who like what I like to find it interesting and sat-isfying too. As for the others, I couldn't please them anyhow, so it is of no use to try. I revise to satisfy myself also — not any imaginary literary critic.

Have you had a classroom or correspondence course on writing fiction? Books on it? To what extent did this help in the elementary stages? Beyond the elementary stages?

L.M. Montgomery: I never took any kind of a course in writing fiction. Such things may be helpful if the real root of the matter is in you, but I had to get along without them. I was born and brought up in a remote country settlement, twenty-four miles from a town and ten from a railway. There I wrote my first stories and my first four books. So no beginner need feel discouraged because of remote location or lack of literary "atmosphere."

How much of your craft have you learned from reading current authors? The classics?

L.M. Montgomery: I think I owe considerable to my greedy reading and rereading of standard fiction — the old masters — Scott, Dickens, Thackeray, Hawthorne. Occasionally, too, a well-written modern magazine story has been helpful and illuminating. But, as a rule, I think aspiring authors will not reap much benefit from current fiction — except perhaps from a purely commercial point of view in finding out what kind of stories certain magazines take! Most writers, except those of absolute genius, are prone to unconscious imitation of what they read and that is a bad thing.

What is your general feeling on the value of technique?

L.M. Montgomery: I feel that its value is great up to a certain point. But when you become conscious of a writer's technique that writer has reached the point of danger. When you find yourself getting more pleasure from the way a writer says a thing than from the thing itself, that writer has committed a grave error and one that lessens greatly the value of his story. Carried too far, technique becomes annoying as mannerisms.

What is most interesting and important to you in your writing — plot, structure, style, material, setting, character, color, etc.?

L.M. Montgomery: In my own writing character is by far the most interesting thing to me — then setting. In the development of the one and the arrangement of the other I find my greatest pleasure and from their letters it is evident that my readers do, too. This, of course, is because my *flair* is for these things. In another writer something else — plot, structure or color would be the vital thing. Only the very great authors combine all these things. For the rank and file of the craft, I think a writer should find out where his strength lies and write his stories along these lines. In my own case I would never attempt to handle complicated plot or large masses of material. I know I should make a dismal failure of them.

What is the elemental hold of fiction on the human mind?

L.M. Montgomery: The deep desire in every one of us for "something better than we have known." In fiction we ask for things, not as they *are*, but as we feel they *ought* to be. This is why the oft-sneered-at "happy ending" makes the popular novel. Fairy tales are immortal — in some form or other we *must* have them or we die. Fiction redresses the balance of existence and gives us what we can't get in real life. This is why "romance" is, and always will be, and always should be more popular than "realism."

Do you prefer writing in the first person or the third? Why?

L.M. Montgomery: Personally I prefer writing in the first person, because it then seems easier to *live* my story as I write it. Since editors seem to have a prejudice against this, I often write a story in the first person and then rewrite it, shifting it to the third. As a reader, I enjoy a story written in the first person far more than any other kind. It gives me more of a sense of reality — of actually knowing the people in it. The author does not seem to *come between* me and the characters as much as in the third-person stories. Wilkie Colliers' *Woman in White* is a fine example of the use of the first person. It could not have been half so effective had he told it in the third. And *Jane Eyre* simply couldn't have been written in any but the first.

Do you lose ideas because your imagination travels faster than your means of recording? Which affords least check — pencil, typewriter or stenographer?

L.M. Montgomery: I don't think many ideas ever get away from me by reason of slowness of recording. My aforesaid note-book habit has been of tremendous value here. I write with a pen and couldn't write with anything else — at least, as far as prose is concerned. When I write verse I always write on an ordinary school slate, because of the facilities for easy erasure. But for prose I want a Waverly pen — this is not an advertisement — I just can't write with any other! a smooth unlined paper and a portfolio I can hold on my knee. Then I can sail straight ahead and keep up with any ideas that present themselves. But these are only personal idiosyncrasies and have nothing to do with a writer's success or non-success. So no aspiring beginner need despair because his or her stationer is not stocked up with Waverly pens!

Famous Author and Simple Mother

*Career and Home Go Together Well For a Woman If She Can Conduct Her
Career at Home, Says L.M. Montgomery, Author of "Anne of Green Gables"
— This Minister's Wife Writes Three Hours Every Morning, No More*

By Norma Phillips Muir

(*The Toronto Star Weekly*, November 28, 1925)

"Make it early Saturday morning, as early as you like," said L.M. Montgomery
(Mrs. Macdonald), author of the "Anne of Green Gables" stories. "I'm going to
take my son downtown for lunch and then on to a movie. He's going to St.
Andrew's now you know. I'm down for his football games."

This was in answer to our plea for half an hour of the time of this busy lady
who combines the career of author with the no less arduous one of minister's
wife and manages to be a pal to her two sons and keep in touch with the ever
turning wheels of the world.

Taking her at her word we were there shortly after nine on the Saturday
morning, but we were not too early for Mrs. Macdonald. She was ready for us,
and had given some time and thought to the matter on which we wanted her
opinion: whether women can successfully possess themselves of careers and
home lives at the same time.

"There are really two answers to that problem," she said smiling. "One is
affirmative and the other is negative. I would say that a woman may successfully combine a profession of her own with the oldest one in the world, that of
wifehood and motherhood, but only if she be able to pursue the career at home.
It doesn't seem to me possible for a mother to be to her children what she
should if they are only the recipients of her left over time, and are, for the major
part under the care of paid help.

"The writing of books, plays, poetry, painting and sculpture — even a career in law is possible and consistent with the duties of wife and mother, but I don't think a woman can pursue any career which takes her away from her home, and still be what she should be to her husband and children. I know there are shining examples where women have been successful in the eyes of the world, and whose homes are supposedly ideally happy, but before I could say that the woman was a success in both phases I'm afraid I should demand the unbiased testimony of her husband and children."

"Think of the great actresses," we protested, "the women who have filled high executive positions, famous women doctors — they have not denied themselves husbands and children. Their very successes have made it possible for them to obtain nurses and governesses for their children — given them care and training which is scientifically perfect, and —"

Has Two Sturdy Sons

"I am thinking," said Mrs. Macdonald quietly. "I'm remembering that the mortality rate in institutions which care for children is infinitely higher than it is in even the poorer class homes. Science is wonderful, but it is not as wonderful for a child as mother-love and mother care. Nothing can make up to a child for that. Children have died, and more will die for love. That is why I say give every woman who wants some interest in addition to her home life a hobby. Give her another interest so that the kitchen and the nursery may not pall, but let it be a hobby, an interest or a profession which she can follow at home."

Then, in answer to our questions Mrs. Macdonald smiled and told us, basing it on her own experiences, of how a woman can have her heart's desire, and no heartburnings and heartsearchings with it.

"The secret really is system," she admitted. "If one doesn't try to run one's life along any definite channels it will soon be like seed sown at random — and the harvest will be too difficult to bring in. Just take that homely old adage, 'A place for everything and everything in its place,' and add to it, 'and a time for everything and everything in its time' and you have the nucleus of success in whatever you are planning to undertake."

We pondered over this for a moment, and then, with a query here, a tentative theory there, the story took form.

It was while she was in her teens that L.M. Montgomery began writing, and like others to whom a large measure of success came later, she made her start in Sunday School papers. Then came serials, followed by "Anne of Green Gables" and with that book came the well deserved laurels. Later on romance, real and not the story book kind, came into the life of the young author, and she married Rev. Ewan Macdonald, and added a home, a husband, the parochial duties of a minister's wife to her authorship. Motherhood was added, and now two sturdy sons tell "mother" their youthful joys and sorrows. Leaskdale and Zephyr are the two charges over which Mr. Macdonald presides, and there are Sunday services, weekday meetings and weeknight gatherings at which the minister and his wife are present, yet L.M. Montgomery's publishers are not disappointed or her public disillusioned when another book from her loved pen appears.

Planning Her Housework

"It does keep me busy," she admitted. "But then there is nothing harder to do than nothing, is there? My day starts at seven in the morning and it lasts until twelve at night. There is breakfast to get, and my younger boy's lunch to pack, routine work to see to — I just have a young maid — and then at nine o'clock I am at my desk and there I stay until twelve. Those three hours a day are all I can allow myself for actual writing, for I am connected with the various church organizations of both charges, president or member or committee worker, and that all takes time. Then there are the countless little things that have to be done about a home to keep it running smoothly, and while I do admit that well trained help could do most of these things as well if not better than the wife and mother can, there is still something about the fact that a man's wife, his sons' mother doing for her family that makes the little acts mean more than if they were twice as efficiently done by someone else. It is the love motif again.

"I think every woman should have an earnest interest outside or rather independent of her home interests, but one which does not take her away from the supervision of her home and the care of her children. The woman who has not children is in another position entirely, but I feel that while a mother is able physically and mentally, the care of her children should not be relegated to outsiders.

"I think there are far too many girls in the world of business today for the good of the world of families," she said quaintly. "Girls have, if they be normal women, a desire for marriage in their hearts, and many of them realize that in the world of business they will have a better opportunity of finding for themselves the type of man they admire, and so — they don't spend the time learning to cook and play the piano and sew and be charming hostesses. They take a commercial course and enter an office and many times defeat their own purposes because the young men they meet are earning not much more than are the girls. They see the girls wearing expensive clothes, appearing well groomed and well content, and when they think, 'there's the kind of girl I'd like to marry,' they stop and think, and the result of the thinking is a decision that it is no use asking her to marry him. How can he suggest that they two get along on what she alone is making now?"

Old Ideals Safe

"Maybe he does ask and she says yes, with the proviso that she keep her position and pay for someone to look after the apartment. Maybe she makes another proviso, or maybe she just makes a resolve to herself, but the fact remains that she keeps her position and he keeps his, and when several Christmases have rolled around there are still no little sox to hang up as an enticement to Santa Claus.

"There are many girls working today who do not need to work, daughters of well-to-do fathers, girls whose mothers need them at home for companionship, but these girls are not content with the dullness and quietness of home. They want to be out in the world of rush and excitement, and so they go, and not being dependent upon what they make, they can afford to work for less, which means that the girl who is her own sole means of support is compelled to take a lower wage in competition with these other girls, and so the economic structure is shaken.

"There is one good thing about to come out of the license and disorder and horror — yes, to mothers and fathers it is horror — of to-day. The motor car, the dance hall, the remote road-houses, and clubs, the petting parties and flask parties — horrible as these are they will have their use, for the pendulum will swing backward again toward decency and normalcy. The girls and boys who are the fastest and the greatest danger to themselves with their desire to be smart and up to date — they are the fathers and mothers of to-morrow, and knowing the dangers that they encountered, the fine line of margin which they took, they will be stricter and more watchful with their children, and so the pendulum will swing backward.

"The secrets of life have been kept too much secrets," said Mrs. Macdonald gravely, "and when these boys and girls, who because they realize that mystery has not paid and so have gone to the other extreme, have reached maturity and parenthood, they will see to it that youth learns the God-purpose of life in a way different from the way in which they learned it, and that the mind and soul and body of their children shall be kept clean and healthy and happy and whole for the joys and purposes of life.

"This has grown to be a far cry from women and their careers in one way," she smiled as we rose to go, "but after all the relationship is close. Give a woman a profession which she will be interested in and devoted to, give it to her within the four walls of her own home and the knowledge that she is not neglecting her home, her husband or her children will give her greater strength and purpose for the career which will be satisfying her need of self expression, and will bring pride to her family, without any of the pain of renunciation."

(Reprinted with permission — The Toronto Star Syndicate.)

The Best Known Woman in Prince Edward Island

By Maude Petitt Hill

Part I: L.M. Montgomery, Author of Anne of Green Gables

(*The Chatelaine*, May 1928)

It was the first morning of our vacation on the North Shore of Prince Edward Island. We were out on the long stretch of sand in the riotous sunshine and sea breeze. Away down a mile or so of wonderfully clean beach, the shore line began to rise abruptly in steep, red sandstone cliffs, finally shutting off the horizon with a ragged bluff.

Every once in a while motors went scudding like quick little black bugs along the top of the cliffs, following a road that wound like a red thread in and out between the land's edge and the green fields.

"Where does that road lead?" we asked a woman from a French fisher home, who happened to be near.

"Dat's de road to Cavendish."

"Cavendish, Cavendish!" Where had we heard of it?

"Oh, isn't that where L.M. Montgomery comes from?" we asked.

"Yes. She's up dere now."

"She's awful good to de people up dere," we elicited after a little querying about her. "Efery Chreesmas she sen' Mrs. W — [12] where she stays, twelve book. She's going to spik in the church to-morrow night."

My young daughters were immediately wild with excitement. To hear the creator of *Anne of Green Gables* actually speak — the author of a book as near their hearts as *Little Women!*

Nor are girls the only readers who appreciate her. Just across from our study window, there lives an old lady of eighty-four, the widow of one of our late Members of Parliament and a real parliamentarian type mentally, herself. Her daughter remarked the other day:

"Do you know, mother still enjoys a book of L.M. Montgomery's just as much as a girl would? We always give her the last one."

There is surely no woman of the Island Province more widely known outside it, and we doubt if any one woman has ever made "The Island," itself, more widely known.

We did not hear that lecture, the proceeds of which were given to the little church at Cavendish. There was a heavy roll from old Neptune that night — it was moonless, too, and the fisherman was afraid we might be driven hard on the rocks in the dark, if we attempted the trip by water. There were only two motors in the little fishing hamlet, and they were otherwise engaged.

But we heard about the lecture from some young people later. What was it on?

"Marco Polo. Marco Polo landed right there at Cavendish!"

"Marco Polo landed at Cavendish?"

"Yes, she said so. Landed right there on the Cavendish sands by her grandfather's farm."

Now, when you are far "frae hame," it is just as well, if you can't believe what the people tell you about another Province, to just take it in polite silence. So did we take *Marco Polo*.

After we came back to Ontario we ran across an article published years ago by L.M. Montgomery on the *Marco Polo*, the fastest sailing vessel of her kind in the world. It had been driven ashore in a gale on the Cavendish sands when the writer was a little girl! The sailors, about twenty of them, had remained in the village for about six weeks and the old Norwegian captain had been a guest in the Montgomery home.

The next week we followed the Bluff Road to the "Anne Country." L.M. Montgomery had gone to her Ontario home again, but we found ourselves in a farm house facing the sea, with a group of women who had grown up with her.

To them she had been little Maud Montgomery, going to the old white-gabled school house.

One almost wishes she had kept that name, Maud Montgomery, for her pen name. It is so euphonious.

We questioned the neighbours eagerly. What did she look like? Was she a clever child, friendly, aloof?

"She was little and thin, with long hair, rather delicate features, and a winning smile," said one.

"Yes, she was rather delicate, but she enjoyed the games, all the same. In fact, she was the life of everything going on."

"She was smart; no trouble for *her* to learn. She was always through her work quickly and then she would be writing stories on her slate. She wrote stories from the time she started school, but only her real friends were let see them. The teachers always thought her very clever."

"Friendly? Yes, and she kept her friends, once she made them. She had a way, though, of going off into sort of dreamy moods. I suppose she was thinking up the things she would be writing later. Her mother, you have probably heard, died when Maud was twenty-one months old. She was raised by her grandmother Macneill in the house beside the church out there. The house has been torn down recently. Tourists passing in the road used to often stop and look at it. She says she remembers being held in her father's arms and looking down into the face of her mother in her coffin."

"Do you suppose she could remember at that age? Don't you think she has heard other people talk of it till she thinks she saw it?" suggested someone.

"Well, she was never like other people," said another woman. "Her mind was always different from the rest of us. It's possible that even in her babyhood she would be able to take in impressions that we could not."

Probably that woman had the correct analysis of the case. The little girl with the highly sensitive mind — the child that could shut her eyes and see things and create people — was no doubt keenly receptive, even in infancy, and was awakened early by the surge of unusual emotion around her in that funeral hour.

To delve into the family history of the Island writer is to explore one of the historic chapters of Canadian life. L.M. Montgomery's ancestors on both sides have lived right there on the North Shore of Prince Edward Island for over a hundred and fifty years. Do we often stop to reflect that we have settlements of such old landed aristocracy? And the story of their coming is a story.

Hugh Montgomery, a paternal ancestor, sailed from Scotland for Quebec. His wife was so desperately sea sick all the way over, that they put her ashore for a little change, near Cavendish, where the vessel hove to for water. And, if you please, the lady refused to set foot off the land again, once she was on it! Expostulation and entreaty were in vain. What could her husband do but stay there with her? So there he settled.

The Macneills, her maternal ancestors, came to Cavendish in 1775. John Macneill had been an adherent of the unfortunate Stuarts and thought it best to change his climate. His son married Eliza Townsend, a daughter of the Captain Townsend who had been given a grant of land at Park Corner, Prince Edward Island, by George III.

But when Grandma Townsend arrived, she was so homesick that family tradition says she paced the floor for three weeks without taking her bonnet off. But she did take her bonnet off finally, raised a family and is there buried in the auld kirk yard at Cavendish.

L.M. Montgomery has said that it is from her mother's people, the Macneills, that she inherits her literary bent. Certainly, they were gifted people, according to Island annals, clever speakers and apt with the pen. John Macneill who came over from Scotland was a brother of Hector Macneill, the author of "Come under Ma Plaidie," often attributed to Burns, and other Scotch songs. John Macneill's eldest son, "Old Speaker Macneill," the great grandfather of L.M. Montgomery, is one of the historic figures of Island Politics.

We have no doubt, too, that the streak of determination handed down from the one grandmother who wouldn't go back on the boat, and that other who refused to take her bonnet off, all helped the subject of our sketch in a career where success is the price of determination against all odds.

It is interesting to see how Providence seems to have prepared for that career and prepared the ideal conditions to foster it. After her mother's death, Maud grew up with her grandparents there in the little Scotch farming community. The quiet farm house was beside the kirk whose long services she squirmed through faithfully from her earliest years.

"I never knew a dull hour in my quiet childhood," she has been heard to say.

Doubtless this was due largely to her gift of imagination. An only child always has certain handicaps in life, but Nature has a wonderful way of balancing things up. Such a child has a particular opportunity for developing any spark of native genius, particularly along literary lines.

When you are a little girl all alone in a house; when there are no other little girls to play with, to eat with, and to sleep with; if you have a spark of imagination, you make little girls of your own — little Floras and Jennies and Annas that run around the house with you in pink aprons and yellow frills. You cuddle up to them at night and talk things over with them as other children do with sisters. You outrun them in the orchard, you dig with them in the sand. But no one ever sees they are there. You wouldn't speak of them to anybody else — no, not for worlds! When L.M. Montgomery conjured up an Anne of Green Gables, she had doubtless just done an old trick over again. We have known only children to make sisters out of sand and water, and put them in the sun to bring them to life, but the dream ones are much more satisfactory.

Not only was the writer's home quiet, but the community about her was exceptionally so. She had never been on a railway train until she was fifteen. You can find girls of fifteen in that quiet Island to-day who have never been on a railway train! But when L.M. Montgomery was five years old she had the thrilling experience of a trip to Charlottetown, driving, of course, a distance of about twenty-five miles!

Nor did the library bring excitement to her ken. There was little or no fiction in the house. "Novels were taboo," she says. "The only ones the library possessed were *The Pickwick Papers*, *Rob Roy* and *Zanoni*."

Magazines were equally scarce, but they did take *Godey's Lady's Book*. She used to peruse the fashion pages, she tells us, and pick out the dresses she would have if she could. But one thing the Macneill home abounded in, and that was poetry. Longfellow, Scott, Tennyson, Whittier, Burns, Byron and Milton all were there. The little girl devoured them eagerly, hungrily.

On Sundays, even poetry was forbidden and, outside the Bible, she was confined to *Pilgrim's Progress* and Talmadge's *Sermons*.

Yet the child's later career was undoubtedly influenced by an early setting of beauty. Down there, where she came out from the break in the sand dunes, was a shore of wild, rugged beauty; red sandstone cliffs reaching upward, one point after another. A few miles away Cape Turner, the highest point in the Island, frowned down upon the sea.

In the opposite direction lay an expanse of clean, smooth, silvery sand, stretching away for miles — the famous Cavendish sands. Along them ran the dunes with their crests of scraggly sand grass; behind the dunes lay the green of fertile farms, orchard bloom, little bits of wood and "The Lake of Shining Waters."

She went berry-picking with the neighbors' children. With "wu'ms" for bait she fished in the trout pond, and even caught a big trout one time. She wandered through orchards and fields and woods. She led a carefree, normal, healthy outdoor life — though not without its childhood sorrows.

One of these, she tells in her own story of her life, was not being allowed to take her lunch to school. The family lived so close to the school house that she had to go home at noon, while the other girls stayed and had a nice, chummy lunch together, and kept their milk cool on a stone in the brook. Another heartbreak was having to wear buttoned boots to school while other children went bare-foot. Little Maud didn't like being "made different," nor the apron that had sleeves in it, which the girls called a "baby apron." No wonder she could write so feelingly in later years, when Anne wanted puffed sleeves such as everybody else wore, and Aunt Marilla wanted her to have straight "sensible ones."

There were thrilling escapades too. There was a place at Cape Leforce (so named because a Captain Leforce had been shot there by his mate), a place where the waves had worn through the red sandstone a little passage as big as a man's hand; then the aperture grew as big as a pumpkin. One of her chums dared her to crawl through. Through the hole she went and her chum went after her. Safely through, they speculated as to what would have happened if they had got stuck in the hole. The waves have since made there a complete channel and a little rock isle.

She had other escapes not so thrilling, but far more real. In her childhood she had typhoid fever. The matter of diet was not considered then. When she began to convalesce she was given a meal of those delicious, highly seasoned, home-made sausages. And medical science to the contrary, she lived to tell the tale!

Then, there were the terrors of the Haunted Wood. She was passionately fond of trees. At nine, she wrote poems about them. But when she was sent a mile down the road to the house where the people sold tea and sugar, and when twilight thickened before she got through the quarter of a mile of woods on the return — those woods were full of creepy things!

It was when she was just nine that she discovered she could write poetry. She read her first attempt to her father.

"Doesn't sound much like poetry," said he.

"Well, it's blank verse."

"Sounds pretty blank," was the crushing criticism.

After that, Maud wrote in rhyme. She wrote stories, too — stories with terrible tragedies; drownings and fires and shootings. She encouraged several of her school mates to branch out along literary lines. She tells of three of them taking the same plot and each writing a story from it. It is rather amusing to think that this same literary stunt is often performed in Writers' Clubs to-day.

At this juncture the young writer began to encounter one of her first difficulties. Her ideas were copious but paper was scarce. The little supply of family note paper was kept sacredly behind the family clock. And what is note paper anyway, to a ready writer?

Here, Fate again took a hand. Her grandfather kept the post office, and she got the "Letter Bills"[13] from the mail bags in which to put forth her first productions. We have heard her say: "I can never bear to see paper wasted, even to this day, because of that scarcity of paper to write on when I was a girl."

While she was not more than twelve, she began to aim at publishing. She sent her first poem to the *Charlottetown Examiner*. She sent several. The thing she omitted to send was postage, not knowing the rules of the game. So the poor child not only did not get her poems printed, but she didn't even get them back!

Up to fifteen she kept on with the struggle. Then came a big change. Her father had married again and settled in Saskatchewan. She took her first ride in a train, to spend a year in a new home. No doubt that year in the West had a great deal to do with the making of the Island authoress.

We never really quite see a place till we get away from it. We cannot get the right perspective. Probably the writer of *Anne of Green Gables* never quite saw her Island home as she saw it from the plains of the West. At any rate, she sent back a poem on Cape Leforce to the *Charlottetown Patriot*, and — she was in print at fifteen! We like to think the West had a hand in her making. It makes her in a double sense Canadian. It was during that year in the West, too, that she entered a story in the prize competition of the Montreal *Witness*, and won. At the end of the year she returned to Cavendish.

Now there is a school in Prince Edward Island without the walls of which no educated Islander is ever properly "finished." One may go to whatever college one likes afterwards! So L.M. Montgomery went to the Prince of Wales College in Charlottetown.

She still further did the then correct thing for an Island girl after graduating — she taught school and taught music. But all the while she wrote.

From teaching, she went to Dalhousie College in Halifax, to take a year's course in English. It was here that occurred her "Big Week." One Monday morning she received from a Philadelphia Sunday School publication the first cheque she had ever received for her writing — five dollars.

Gloves, scarves, things a girl would like? No; she liked all those well enough, but she went down town and bought five books, something she could always keep: Tennyson, Byron, Milton, Longfellow and Whittier.

On Wednesday she received a prize of five dollars from the Halifax *Evening Mail* for the best letter on the subject, "Which Has the Greater Patience — Man or Woman?" On Saturday, she received a cheque from *The Youth's Companion* for ten dollars. Three cheques in one week! It was almost too much.

She went back from Dalhousie to Prince Edward Island and taught again. If she had written before, she was possessed now, though the conditions under which she lived were far from conducive to writing.

She boarded in a very cold farmhouse. Her schoolwork was so strenuous that she was too tired to write at night; but she managed to get up religiously at six A.M. and dress by lamplight before the fires were lighted. She would put on a heavy coat and sit on her feet to keep them from freezing. With fingers blue with cold, she used to struggle to write her stint for the day. Then she thawed out her hands, ate breakfast and went out to teach "the young idea how to shoot."

A little later came another change in her life. Her grandfather died in 1898, and her grandmother was left alone in the old homestead. She promptly gave up teaching and stayed at home with her, devoting all her spare time to writing.

"By 1901," she has been heard to say, "I was beginning to make a 'livable' income for myself by my pen, though that did not mean that everything I wrote was accepted on its first journey — far from it. Nine out of ten manuscripts came back to me. But I sent them out over and over again, and eventually they found resting places."

It was not a life that would lure most girls in the early twenties who had tasted a little of the world, that quiet life in her grandmother's home. But it was her duty, and she was Scotch! So there for thirteen years she stayed, with the exception of one year spent as a proof reader on the *Halifax Daily Echo*. That year, no doubt, gave her a valuable and helpful experience, but we believe it was those silent twelve years that gave us her books.

The clock ticked in the still house; the cat slept on the cushion in the big, old chair; and the red-haired Anne came suddenly out of the dark corners of the old house. On one occasion when we heard the author speak in Toronto, she said:

"I didn't create Anne. She just was suddenly there, name with the 'E' and all."

There was a certain newspaper clipping[14] that Miss Montgomery had brought home with her from Halifax: "Elderly couple apply to orphan asylum for a boy. By mistake a girl is sent them." The girl and the clipping went together like that.

Maud had brought home also an old typewriter. It wouldn't make an "M" or clean capitals, but with these minor handicaps, she managed to type her manuscript. She sent it out for the first time to a new firm, thinking it might stand a better chance. The new firm returned it. She then sent it to an old established firm. The old established firm returned it. She sent it out a third time. A third time it came back!

"If we hadn't kept the post office," she once said, "I don't believe I'd have been a writer. I couldn't have endured having some one else see me getting my manuscripts back all the time."

She sent Anne out a fourth time. A fourth time she returned. She sent her off the fifth time. This time, when she came back, the publisher said his reader "found some merit in the story, but not enough to warrant its publication."

This was too much. The writer carried her red-haired child up to the store room in the attic. With tightly closed lips she laid her high hopes away in an old empty hat box.

Part II: L.M. Montgomery, After Her First Success
(*The Chatelaine*, June, 1928)

Spring housecleaning nearly always brings some neglected thing to light. The snow was lingering on the hills of Cavendish when L.M. Montgomery decided to go up to the attic one wintry afternoon and do a little of what housekeepers call "ridding up," preparatory to the spring cleaning.

Back there, in the farthest corner of the store room under the gabled roof, was that old hat box. She pulled it out. Oh, yes, the manuscript of *Anne of Green Gables*! Poor Anne, child of her dream — spurned by five publishing houses!

Well, Anne was evidently not destined for the world of book shelves in a pretty coat of red or green cloth. One more hope to the ground! Small wonder if she felt as Anne herself did when she found they had really sent for a boy at Green Gables, and weren't likely to keep her: "My life is a perfect graveyard of buried hopes."

But, at any rate, she could cut the manuscript down to a six or seven-chapter serial for a juvenile paper. It meant a good deal of work, and she would only get thirty-five or forty dollars for it. But she ought to do something with it. It had lain there neglected for a year.

She took it out and began to read from the beginning. She read on and on. The sun sank lower behind the hills — its rays were running level through the gable window across the attic floor. Suddenly she started up. Gracious! The afternoon had slipped away! Time to look after the tea. She had read nearly all the afternoon like a school girl and forgotten all about the work she came up to do!

But still she paused, a queerish new light in her eyes. "If your own story could interest you after you have laid it away, until it made you forget all about your work like this — wouldn't it interest other people if it were printed," whispered something.

A few days later the would-be authoress tied up *Anne of Green Gables* and sent her off again to Boston, this time to the L.C. Page Company.

It was natural for a Prince Edward Island girl to send her manuscript to Boston rather than Montreal or Toronto, even if she had been rebuffed there before. All Maritime province ambition turns to Boston. The farmer's daughter is educated for a teacher or trained for a nurse and goes to Boston. The fisherman's daughter goes to Boston to get high pay in housework. The sons everywhere go there to try their wings in the world of commerce. A very large percentage of the professional men of Massachusetts are natives of our Maritimes. When the people of the Maritime Provinces take a long trip, they go to Boston — very seldom to Montreal or Toronto.

Nevertheless, it was well that, with its millions of readers, Boston should get *Anne of Green Gables* on her sixth excursion. She passed through the hands of the manuscript readers and came, finally, to the publisher himself. And then, one more perverse publisher decided to reject *Anne of Green Gables*. Possibly the manuscript was a little dog-eared after its five previous excursions, and its year in the hat box. Undoubtedly, it had a sort of hang-dog look.

At any rate, over among the manuscripts to be tied up for return, went *Anne*. But there was one factor on which the publisher had not counted. One of his manuscript readers was a girl from Prince Edward Island. Now the "Islanders" are intensely loyal to one another. It is said they never quite learn to think of any other place as home.

Into the office of the chief, entered the irate young Island reader when she learned of the manuscript's fate. She had its points all down pat. She had made up her mind to camp right there by the desk of L.C. Page until he said he would publish *Anne of Green Gables*. And camp there she did, and argued and argued and argued, until the publisher, being only a man after all, surrendered!

L.M. Montgomery never knew the true story of her book's acceptance until years after, when she heard it through a travelling salesman. All she knew then was that one afternoon the sunshine at Cavendish became all aglitter, because she had opened a letter from Boston saying her book was accepted for publication.

In her journal at that time, she wrote: "The book may or may not succeed. I wrote it for love not money; but very often such books are the most successful, just as everything in the world that is born of true love has life in it as nothing constructed for mercenary ends can ever have. The dream dreamed years ago, at that old brown desk in school has come true at last after years of toil and struggle. And the realization is sweet, almost as sweet as the dream."

Her idea of the success of her book had been, from her own confession, a very limited one. She had thought it would be read by girls of teen age. She had never dreamed that its sale would, according to her present publisher, touch the million mark; that premiers and princes would one day seek her out and shake her hand.

It was not until the year after its acceptance that the book was published. On June 20th, 1908, she wrote in her journal:

> "To-day has been, as Anne herself would say, 'an epoch in my life.' My book came to-day, 'spleet new' from the publishers. I candidly confess that it was to me a proud and wonderful and thrilling moment. There, in my hand, lay the material realization of the dreams, hopes, ambitions and struggles of my whole conscious existence — my first book. Not a great book, but mine, mine, mine — something which I had created."

Nor did the thrills end with that moment. As the sales mounted there were letters coming to the young writer from all parts of the world, not only from the children, who believed that Anne was real, but from gray-haired grandfathers, boys at college, pioneers in the Australian bush. The English public particularly responded to this simple life-story of the girl on a Canadian farm. But, of course, it was the American sales that swelled her royalties. Mark Twain described Anne as "the sweetest creation of child-life yet written."[15] Bliss Carman also voiced his appreciation. And, if the sight of the American copy of her story had thrilled its author, what must it have meant to see a Swedish and also a Dutch copy appearing. The *Truro Weekly* said of the book that it had definitely fixed its author's place "as the Jane Austen of Canadian literature."

In 1909, following her big success, L.M. Montgomery had no difficulty in publishing her second book, *Anne of Avonlea*, and the following year *Kilmeny of the Orchard*. This was really an earlier work of hers, first published as a serial. Consequently, she was rather amused when a reviewer remarked of it that the book showed "the insidious influence of popularity and success."

The following year, came *The Story Girl*, a replica of Prince Edward Island scenery and life as it was around her, the last of L.M. Montgomery's books to be written there by her window under the gabled roof.

The writer had been continuing her quiet life in these pastoral scenes, playing the organ of the little church, teaching in the Sunday School, bearing her share of the little neighborhood doings as though the literary circles of big cities had never beckoned her. There came into her community one day to preach, however, one, the Reverend Ewan Macdonald. He it was, who was destined, a little later, to lure her from her beloved island.

In the winter of 1911, Grandmother Macneill died at the age of eighty-seven. There ended thirteen years of faithful care of one who had herself cared for the author from babyhood.

In the summer of that year, Lucy Maud Montgomery was married from her uncle's house at Park Corner, a few miles away, to the Rev. Ewan Macdonald, then in charge of the Presbyterian church at Leaskdale, Ont. They left immediately to spend their honeymoon in the British Isles.

We get a little glimpse of how deeply embedded in Mrs. Macdonald's nature is her love of home, when speaking of walking on the Spittal Shore by moonlight, she says: "It was beautiful, but so like the Cavendish Shore that it made me bitterly homesick."

In a London antique shop she picked up a pair of spotted china dogs for her new home, which reminded her of a funny incident of her childhood.

In her uncle's house at Park Corner there were two spotted china dogs on the mantel. When she was a little girl her father had told her that whenever those dogs heard the clock strike midnight they would bounce down on the rug and bark. She had thenceforth pleaded to be let stay up till midnight. But her elders were obdurate in refusing.

However, one night she discovered that the dogs didn't bark at twelve, and her faith in her father's truthfulness was badly shattered. But he restored it somewhat by explaining that he had said "whenever the dogs *heard* the clock strike they would bark!" but china dogs never heard.

Back to their new home in the Manse at Leaskdale, Ontario came the bride and groom some sixteen years ago. As they passed through Toronto, the Women's Press Club of that city held a reception in the King Edward Hotel in honor of Mrs. Macdonald and Mrs. Macgregor (Marion Keith), also a bride.

Then Mrs. Macdonald settled to her life in the village manse, where two little sons, Chester and Stuart, were born.

When the elder was a baby, his mother took him to visit Prince Edward Island. By way of welcome, the Charlottetown paper that had rejected her poems in her youth, announced oddly that Miss Montgomery and her infant son were staying at the Hotel in that city. Such is fame!

During those years in Leaskdale Manse, Mrs. Macdonald has added steadily to her list of books. Anne, who had passed through the adopted orphan stage, the college and school teaching stage, reached the doctor's wife period in *Anne's House of Dreams*, she raised her family in *Rainbow Valley*, after which her girlish vagaries were taken up by Rilla, her youngest born.

In *Rilla of Ingleside*, L.M. Montgomery has preserved a perfect little picture of the social and home life of her Island during the days of the war. If Anne had not been so famous, possibly Rilla would have had a bigger place on the stage. But like Adam, Anne came first.

Then Emily took the field as a child, and *Emily of New Moon* was pronounced by some reviewers the writer's best book since *Anne of Green Gables*. Undoubtedly, L.M. Montgomery is at her best in writing about children.

It is perhaps for the best that her own children have been sons, not daughters. Girls would have had a hard time holding their own with these dream girls of her fancy.

By reason of the fact that Emily has, in her later books, *Emily Climbs* and *Emily's Quest*, developed into a writer, she is perhaps less popular than if she had followed an ordinary walk in life. One of the rest of us might picture herself filling it, then! For after all, a story about a writer doesn't appeal to such a large class as one about a fisherman's wife or a farmer's daughter.

In *Blue Castle* the writer made a very successful excursion into Ontario life, lighted by the scenery of Muskoka.

With her youth in the Maritimes, her year in the West and her married life in Ontario, she is truly a well-rounded Canadian writer.

After all, the best way to know a writer is not to read a biographical sketch of her life, but to read something she has written. Some one once said to a young writer, of people who said they knew her through her writing:

"They know you as you write. We know you as you are."

"No," said the writer quickly, "they who read me know me as I am. You, who live with me, know me as I seem."

One likes to read L.M. Montgomery as she has expressed herself in her poetry. For besides her fourteen works of fiction, she has published a book of poems, *The Watchman*. Here is a bit from its closing stanza where Maximus speaks:

> *"I care no more for glory; all desire*
> *For conquest and for strife is gone from me,*
> *All eagerness for war; I only care*
> *To help and heal bruised beings and to give*
> *Some comfort to the weak and the suffering.*

I cannot even hate those Jews; my lips
Speak harshly of them, but within my heart
I feel a strange compassion; and I love
All creatures, to the vilest of the slaves,
Who seem to me as brothers."

Or, in a shorter poem —

"The wind has grown too weary for a comrade;
It is keening in the rushes, spent and low.
Let us join our hands and hasten very softly,
To the little olden friendly path we know."

In another —

"Dear God our life is beautiful
*   In every splendid gift it brings;*
But most I thank thee humbly for
*   The joy of little things."*

And the description of dawn on the seashore —

"Across the ocean wan and gray
*   Gay fleets of golden ripples come,*
For at the birth hour of the day
*   The roistering wayward winds are dumb.*
The rocks that stretch to meet the tide
*   Are smitten with a ruddy glow.*
And faint reflections come and go,
*   Where fishing boats at anchor ride."*

Her poetry, like her fiction, reflects her Island shores. Doubtless one of the great secrets of L.M. Montgomery's success as a writer, has been that she was artist enough to paint the simple every day life about her childhood home. We once heard an editor say that one of the greatest shortcomings among writers was that a man sitting in a steam-heated flat wanted to write stories about trapping polar bears. L.M. Montgomery has never strayed from the paths she herself knew.

A "bit sentimental," some librarians have called her books. Yes, but after all, isn't that part of her fidelity to the life she is picturing? When you are writing the lives of young girls in uneventful rural districts one has to remember that simple love affairs crop up like daisies in the meadows. In her particular province, young girls marry early and settle down faithfully. The province has known but one divorce since the days of Confederation! In all probability, too, the girls of a decade ago *were* more sentimental.

At any rate, the sentiment in these books is wholesome, and we believe that this latter is another of the reasons why L.M. Montgomery's books have had such a wide sale. After all, the majority of us, when we buy a book for the family shelf, we are apt to select books that, as one reviewer put it, "deal with pleasant people in a pleasant way."

People find something refreshing in the stories from this land where, as we once heard the writer say, "nearly every family still hopes the eldest son will be a minister and it would be a disgrace to have company catch one without three kinds of cake in the house."

When I visited Prince Edward Island last summer, I watched for that three kinds of cake — and do you know, at every table where we sat down, we always found the three varieties?

Another of the keys with which L.M. Montgomery has unlocked the door of success is that she lives life as well as she writes. Down there on the Island where she spends her holidays every other summer, people tell you the kindnesses she has done in passing — the books given the schools; the pictures hung on the school room wall; the lecture given for the funds of the little church; the delicate girl taken from some farm home back with her to Ontario.

And from all accounts she has continued the same sort of life in Ontario. She helps in the Sunday School, the Woman's Missionary Society, and the Young People's work. About four years ago the Macdonalds moved from Leaskdale to the Manse at Norval, Ont. about twenty miles from Toronto. When we saw Mrs. Macdonald at the time of preparing this article, she explained, "I'm rushed just now, helping the young people with two plays they are putting on in our two churches."

"How do you manage to write in a Manse?" we asked.

"Oh, it isn't any harder to write in a Manse than any other place," she said. "I set apart three hours a day for writing." "I don't think her home has ever known neglect from her writing," said one who knew her intimately.

Her sons, Chester and Stuart, are now fifteen and twelve years of age. They are in St. Andrew's College at Aurora, not far from the Norval Manse. When they were "wee bairns," a guest tells us, they used to shove flowers under the door into the room where their mother was writing.

There is a nice big furry cat, named "Lucky" in the Manse. If you don't meet Lucky you won't have met all the family, for as his mistress explains, he is "almost human." Four years ago, as a kitten, he travelled all alone in a box from Prince Edward Island. "Lucky" was well named, I thought. I recalled a simple sentence L.M. Montgomery had added, seemingly rather irrelevantly, to an address some years ago: "And I always like a cat in the room when I'm writing!"

Many honors have come to the writer since the publication of her first book. She was the first Canadian woman to be made a Fellow of the Royal Society of Arts and Literature of Great Britain. When Premier Baldwin and the Prince of Wales were making their Canadian tour last summer, the Premier requested that it be arranged for him to meet the Canadian writer whose stories he had so much enjoyed. In consequence, when the reception was held for the Premier and the Prince at the Lieutenant-Governor's in Toronto, he made her acquaintance. Nor had he forgotten his request.

When one of the officers learned her name on her arrival, he said, "Oh, yes, the Premier has been asking if you had arrived."

In his address at Charlottetown on his return journey, Premier Baldwin told the Prince Edward Islanders how he had enjoyed the works of their "own authoress."

Earl Grey, too, during his regime in Canada, visited her in Prince Edward Island, to express his appreciation of her work.

But of all the honors paid her, perhaps the simplest and the sweetest is the way in which her own Island people welcome you to their homes. When you enter their houses, they thrust forward for you "the chair L.M. Montgomery sat in, when she was here."

Minister's Wife and Authoress

By C.L. Cowan

(*The Toronto Star Weekly*, December 29, 1928)

Twenty years ago I arrived in this land of promise, Canada. At that time two names loomed large on the literary horizon, that of Ralph Connor (Rev. C.W. Gordon, D.D.), whose domicile was in Winnipeg, the gateway of the far west, and that of L.M. Montgomery, who claimed the far east as her home. Ralph Connor swung into ken by his stirring tales of lumberjacks and rivermen, sky pilots and cowmen; L.M. Montgomery by her delightful, wholesome "Anne"[16] series that depicted a life that profoundly differed in outlook and practice from the former. It was natural that both should find a ready sale for their works for the fields explored were virgin and the writers excellent exponents of their craft. It must be a matter of considerable gratification to each of them that their products are still among Canada's best-sellers, and that each new book from their respective pens is signalled as an event in the literary world.

Some weeks ago the Presbyterian ministers of our city and their wives decided to have a banquet and the speaker chosen was L.M. Montgomery (Mrs. Ewan Macdonald), the manse, Norval, Ontario. She was invited to our home. I had had much experience of ministers' wives (I have lived with one for sixteen years) from Ontario to British Columbia and found them to be noble, self-sacrificing homemakers, hard-working, unpaid curates to their husbands almost without exception; but this was a new experience to meet a literary celebrity who was also a parson's wife. Just a short time before I had read that the Prince of Wales and Premier Baldwin of Great Britain desired to see her when in this country and that she had responded. Mr. Baldwin, according to newspaper report, had declared that one of his anticipated joys on coming to Canada was to meet L.M. Montgomery, the author of one of his favorite books, "Anne of

Green Gables." So it was with some trepidation that we awaited our distin-guished guest. Authors are generally reputed to have certain peculiarities, born with them or diligently acquired. One literary genius never knew, never cared about meal hours. Bah! To eat food was a mundane exercise fit only for the common herd! Another was so absent-minded that not until his humiliated wife informed him did he know that he had joined in the applause that fol-lowed a speech he had made.

First Book Ran 500,000

However, we need not have been in any way perturbed over the coming of our guest. She quickly made herself at home, and ere many minutes had passed we were comfortably seated about a cheery fire talking like old friends.

She is a comely, comfortable looking lady. The years have dealt kindly with her; she still retains a fair share of her youthful looks, and the fine color swept into her cheeks by the wind of the north shore of Prince Edward Island still adorns her kindly face. Presently I steered the conversation round to her books. She had written fourteen, the last one being just forwarded to her publishers. "The Magic of Marigold" should have a fine reception.

As "Anne of Green Gables" is perhaps her best-known work, I inquired as to its circulation, and her guess was around 500,000. This must be near to a record for a Canadian story. Just recently I observed that R.E. Knowles, who has an admiring following in *The Toronto Star*, admitted proudly that his "St. Cuthbert's" had reached the 100,000 mark. Perhaps Connor's "Sky Pilot" has reached more readers than "Anne of Green Gables," but I have not heard.

A singular analogy exists in the matter of Sir Walter Scott's "Waverley" and "Anne of Green Gables" in that Sir Walter had thrown aside the manu-script of "Waverley" and apparently had forgotten all about it until he discov-ered it when he was searching for some fishing tackle. "Anne of Green Gables," too, appears to have been cast into the limbo of forgotten things, for L.M. Montgomery found the M.S. in an old trunk or attic and decided that publishers would be given the privilege of looking it over.[17] The results were unanticipated and gratifying, as the figures above reveal.

The publishing of books, especially first books, is largely a gamble. Somewhere I read that out of every thousand books printed six hundred never pay the cost of printing, two hundred just pay expenses, one hundred return a small profit and the remainder show a substantial profit. If these figures are approximately correct, publishing firms assume no small risk when they send forth a new volume. No wonder the colorful "jacket" has become a feature of astute modern book salesmanship. "Anne of Green Gables" came on to the retail counters of booksellers in the days when the aforementioned "clothing" was unthought of, and was almost immediately a bestseller. It had the guinea stamp!

New Generation is O.K.

Since L.M. Montgomery's appeal is very largely to the young women of to-day, it was natural that she should be asked concerning them. "What is your opinion of girls of this so-called fast age?" she was queried. Her reply was definite, unhesitating: "Just as good as those of any other generation. There is a certain proportion of 'high-fliers' in every generation — the ages do not differ radically. Girls are freer to express themselves now. The pressure is off: that is about all the difference there is between our girls now and those of a bygone day."

"And so you think that the much-powdered and puffed, compacted and barbered, gay and daring young ladies of the present, generally speaking, will ultimately settle down to the humdrum business of marriage and all responsibilities it entails?"

A decided "I do" came from the famous novelist's lips. And as one who has had abundant opportunities for seeing the matter tested out I can corroborate L.M. Montgomery's opinion. Between thirty-five and forty brides stand before me yearly with their grooms. I visit a goodly proportion of their homes afterwards. With ninety-nine percent of them the little home is the paramount interest. Canada, I hardly imagine, need not be unduly worried over the nurs-eries of to-day and to-morrow.

One could see that Mrs. E. Macdonald — or L.M. Montgomery as the world prefers to call her — is a proud mother. She has two fine boys attending St. Andrew's College near Toronto. A rather embarrassing notice was printed in the society column of a way-down-east newspaper a year or two after her marriage. She told it against herself with glee. This paper announced that Miss. L.M. Montgomery had arrived in the town for a visit with her young son! Her interest extends to the sports of her lads. We can imagine the tender pride that would light up her face when an extra letter came from one of them with the breath-taking news that he had made the rugby team!

The address of our guest to the Presbyterian ministers of Hamilton was informative and piquant. She told a few thrilling stories of a day that is swiftly passing down in Prince Edward Island. My interest centred in her literary rem-iniscences. The mail carries to her most interesting letters. They come from all parts of the world.

A Long Lost Uncle

In Australia, perhaps, she has as many admirers as anywhere else. There her books have the greatest sale in proportion to the population. A mother superi-or in an Australian convent in a letter expressed her thanks for the clean, inspiring note that runs through her books, and expressed the thought that the writer should be a Catholic. The lady further communicated to L.M. Montgomery that every night she knelt in the chapel and prayed that she might come to the light some day.

"I will tell you," confessed the speaker, "that her letter touched me deeply. It is something to know that one person in the world prays for me."

When "Anne of Green Gables" was first published under the name she continues to write under, a reader wrote to express her joy that she had found a lost relative. The letter began, "My dear long-lost uncle!" L.M.

Montgomery was the name of the wandering uncle. The novelist was sorry to disillusion the correspondent.

Not all the letters received by L.M. Montgomery are so pleasant. She has not escaped the criticism of the "uncoguid." Although no modern novelist, man or woman, is more careful in the materials that go to make up her stories, the very fact that she has allowed some of her male characters to court the goddess Nicotine brought wrath upon her. Her answer to one of these detractors was a reminder that probably the "Iliad" would not have been written had Helen been a perfect character, and had not Lucifer fallen, the blind Milton would not have given to the world his incomparable "Paradise Lost." But this woman was not to be denied a come-back. She countered with the remark that it would be better to write dull books free from the taint of evil than interesting books smudged with "vice."

I had the pleasure of joining in moving a motion of thanks to L.M. Montgomery, and in the course of my remarks I confessed that my first story, a three-column affair, gained for me the magnificent sum of three dollars! When she responded she drew a laugh by confessing that her first literary effort was not so well rewarded. A florists' trade magazine printed her initial verses, and she was permitted, as a reward, to pick out seeds to the value of fifty cents! "I picked them out," she said, "and planted them in my garden. There was a riot of color for my pains. I have often wished that every ten lines I wrote since that time brought me as much happiness as those ten lines for which I got the seeds."

Every writer, I suppose, has the same thing to confess that there is no joy just quite like that of first breaking into print, and no reward quite as significant as the first, no matter how poor it may appear in comparison with later financial success.

L.M. Montgomery has plans for the future. She hopes some day to step out into the adult field, to write for a more mature class of readers (although even now she does not lack them) than she has done for so long. She has the ability and the temperament to do so, and a host of readers throughout the world will look for a new venture on her part confident that success will be the outcome.

Poetry Her First Love Says L.M. Montgomery

Revealing Glimpse of Canadian Writer Given by Herself.

(*The Mail and Empire*, March 19, 1929)

"Poetry was my first love, and I have always regretted being false to it. But one must live," says L.M. Montgomery, author of *Anne of Green Gables*, and fifteen other entertaining books, writing autobiographically in the current issue of *The Ontario Library Review*.

Miss Montgomery, who is Mrs. Ewan Macdonald in private life, tells an amusing story of her first adventure into poetry. She had been revelling in Tennyson, Byron, Scott, Milton, Burns. And one wonderful day when she was nine years old she discovered that she could write "poetry" herself.

"It was called 'Autumn,' and I wrote it on the back of an old post-office letter bill (she relates) for writing paper was not too plentiful in that old farmhouse, where nothing was ever written save an occasional letter. I read it aloud to father. Father said it didn't sound much like poetry. 'It's blank verse,' I cried. 'Very blank,' said father."

She then determined that her next poem should rhyme, and wrote yards of verses about flowers and months and trees and stars and sunsets and address lines to her friends. When she was 13 she began sending verses to the Prince Edward Island weekly paper — and confesses she never heard either of or from them. "Perhaps this was because I did not send any return stamps — being then in blissful ignorance of such a requirement."

Then she turned to prose and says that the editor of a U.S. juvenile magazine "accepted" a short story and enclosed a check "for five whole dollars."

"Never in all my life have I felt so rich as I did then!" goes on the creator of all the Annes. "Did I spend it for needed boots and gloves? I did not. I wanted to get something I could keep forever in memory of having arrived. I hied me down town and purchased leather-bound dollar editions of Milton, Byron, Wordsworth, Longellow and Tennyson. I have repented me of many things rashly bought in my life, but never of those. I have them yet — dingy and shabby now — but with the springs of eternal life still bubbling freshly in them. Not that I do not love many modern poets. I do. But the old magic was good and remains good."

L.M. Montgomery as a
Letter Writer

By Ephraim Weber[18]

(*The Dalhousie Review*, October 1942)

Ten years ago it was my privilege to introduce L.M. Montgomery to an audience of her readers. In opening her address, she said that she and I had exchanged literary letters for thirty years, though we had never met until the year before, and that, of her many literary correspondents of old, a friend in England and I were the only ones still on her list. This was news to me. And why we two? Were we bolder to strain her good nature, or more patient to decipher her long letters? I hardly dared think we wrote *better* letters. I never found out. In any case, she could easily have squelched us with silence. Of the other survivor I am sorry to know nothing, but as for me, the exchange has been richly in my favor, aside from the honor of it. Surely a famous author needs no obscure schoolmaster.

My respects to L.M. Montgomery's memory are herewith to take form in a few confessions, in which the aim is to show her excellence in the lost and lovely art of letter-writing. As her books are so charming, what may her letters be like? What did she write about, and how? Yes, you are right: her epistolary style carried her personality to her distant friends, for in her case decidedly the style was the man.

Scribbling a bit for second-rate periodicals in my young days, I noticed now and again a "yarnlet" or a snippet of poetry by one L.M. Montgomery, whom by a funny freak I fancied a whiskered sage, "goodly in girth," one whose thinking and rhyming powers were being liberated into appealing utterance. Trying to do something similar, I was wishing to get in touch with him, but hesitated to write to one of the publishers for his address; "I'd never hear from him anyway."

One day a letter came from a fellow-scribbler in Philadelphia, a stranger, who fancied some little thing of mine in a periodical. In answering I mentioned L.M.

Montgomery, whoever he was, as one of my new discoveries in current literature. A reply soon came from Philadelphia with the Montgomery address, urging me to write to my new Canadian writer-friend — "You'll hear from this kindred spirit."

I wrote. In due time a letter came from Cavendish, Prince Edward Island, signed Lucy Maude Montgomery! It was a shattering jolt. By instant alchemy the whiskers vanished, and the goodly girth assumed fashionplate length and lankness, but there was now an intellectual nose and a "mild and magnificent eye."

The twentieth century had just seen daylight, and for forty years, up to her illness many months ago, this revised L.M. Montgomery answered my letters with epistles I call classics.

My correspondent's image was changed a second time — how agreeably! — when some years later I saw her picture in a magazine. The lankness shrank into a short and less bony figure; the eye was still magnificent, but now it was the *brow* that was intellectual.

The early Cavendish letters, unlike the later ones, came in ordinary envelopes with single postage. They contained chatty accounts of their writer's activities in the simple life of her Island, her love of cats and flowers and woods and lonely seashore walks at dusk, but mainly of her literary doings: lyric bits in humble monthlies, young people's weeklies, and later, in the *Sunday School Times* of Philadelphia. Many a "faith trip" some of them made before they found asylum in printer's ink. There was constant exploring for new markets, and during her year in Halifax there were sallies for news stories and for the *Halifax Echo*. These letters told of ways and means and little helps in the art of writing, gave nerving thoughts on the pain of rejections, and recommended bee-like assiduity in gathering material. They reported how courteous some editors were, and how heartless others; which publications paid on acceptance (only they seldom accepted), and which ones kept your manuscript "on the ticklish balance of suspense" till you were sure they'd print it; then when it was out of season, returned it with those polite regrets in stereotyped print. Such were the chronicles of that dawn time.

Even so, there was hardly ever a letter that had no triumph over the Powers of Rejection to tell of. A triumph was a cheque for five, three, and even two dollars.

In a few more years the lengthening Montgomery letters told of more frequent acceptances with better pay. Montgomery poems were now seen in such classic print as *Youth's Companion*; Montgomery stories occasionally got into the better magazines, Canadian and American. Whenever, in the remoteness of my homestead near the foothills of the Rockies, I did not have access to the publication containing a sample of my friend's work, she would send me a copy, either of the periodical or of the piece in her own hand. Of course I would report my impressions, hardly ever finding any faults worth showing off my acumen, but it was a delight to dwell on the merits. If it was a poem, what fine fresh fancies, and how her rhymes and metres sang around her similes and metaphors! L.M. Montgomery had a lovely lyric knack.

When one of her letters announced she was writing a book, "Great Scott and Caesar's Ghost!" my thoughts exclaimed. "A book! What shall I do now?" I was afraid to read on, lest I might learn she could now get along without my letters. A book! Why, that made an author of her, and authors have no time for the common herd.

No, it made no difference; she retained me.

Still, I had misgivings about the future: some day her completed book would make her famous. I wished her no harm, ye gods! but when she wrote that her manuscript of *Anne of Green Gables* had been rejected five times, the foundation of my hope seemed to contain more cement. A few months later a letter announced that *Anne* was sold to one of the major American publishers. Even to me that was a thriller. Such an achievement made common drudges of the Empire Builders. But would I survive? "Oh, well, perhaps the book won't be a big success," my evil angel comforted in a timid whisper. But *Anne* crashed the gates to the big sellers, outstripped some of them, in fact: spilled over into England, France, Poland, Spain and Finland! Read in five languages, she wore "the million halo." All this I quizzed from her modest creator. Some years later she told me her book was printed in a language one wouldn't guess — braille.

And still it made no difference in my mail: eighteen to thirty largepad loosely-written pages of personal news and views. I never felt I was quite entitled to such expansive, fraternizing responses, happy as I was to get them.

More *Anne* books came along: *Anne of Avonlea*, *Anne of Ingleside*, *Anne of the Island*, *Anne's House of Dreams*, *Anne of Windy Poplars*; also the *Emily* books and the *Pat* books, *Marigold*, *Kilmeny*, *The Story Girl*, *The Tangled Web*, *Rainbow Valley* and several others. After the first dozen were out, I felt middling safe, for not even then was there the least deadness in the letters, never a perfunctory line.

If my Montgomery missives have in late years become annuals, they have been requiring indemnifying double fare on the long envelopes. For intimacy, for conversational effect, for stimulating play of thought, one long epistle is surely worth a walletful of hasty notes. The day of long letters has gone with the horse and buggy, but the author of the *Anne's* and the *Emily* has preserved the liberal epistolary ways of the Queen Anners and the Victorians.

L.M. Montgomery always told me what book she was getting ready next for her world, and whenever she had one published she sent me an autographed copy. A letter announced she had for months been on an adult novel. A Montgomery story that wasn't a girls' novel! What might that be like? The next letter said it was nearly done. Curiosity became suspense. Six months later along it came, in Hodder and Stoughton format: *The Blue Castle*, autographed by the author.

It was avidly read. My wife always read out Montgomery stories to me. We had got to Valancy's marriage proposal to Barney, when, laying the book down to laugh, she caught sight of the flopping leaves, and with an excited voice bade me "Look here!" There on a front page I read:

> To Mr. Ephraim Weber, M.A.,
> Who understands the architecture of Blue Castles.

What? We both scrutinized and made sure. So the new kind of Montgomery fiction was dedicated to me! What for? What had I done, or been? And how could I be said to understand the architecture of Blue Castles when I hardly knew what they were? It demanded a reperusal of the volume with interpretative intent, as well as an enquiry in my next letter. The Oracle answered:

You, like most people of the House of Joseph, understand
"how fair the realms imagination opens to the view."

It was long ago that our letters quit talking shop, for I practically neglected my writing. But there was plenty we exchanged about literature, standard and current, religion and the churches, education and the schools, the changing moral standard (only "it isn't changing," said my friend), the new rising generation (only "it isn't new," she declared), the warless world ("not *this* one ever," she countered).

In talking on serious topics, people seldom give each other time to finish their speeches; but when one party is at Cavendish, P.E.I., the other at Didsbury, Alberta, four-fifths of the continent between, it is not so hard to keep from interrupting. Another advantage of conversing by letter is that we have time to think out better speeches. Once I gave a wee disquisition on the moral constitution of the universe, culminating with this: "We are not punished *for* our sins, but *by* them." The reply had a wee disquisition on the nature of the Bible, culminating with this: "I do not believe the Bible is inspired *by* God, but *with* God." So we exchanged wisdom and epigram, perhaps not so original as we then thought; but so we kept our intellectual souls in clover when the local pickings were scant at either end.

After thirty years of this paper conversing, we met. We almost called for pen and ink! The face-to-face way wasn't the same thing.

What is the source of charm in letters of friendship? Is it that the absence of the physical person stimulates the creation of the friend's ideal personality? And anyway, as absence makes the heart grow fonder, the suspense of anticipating letters almost makes golden texts of half the sentences.

II.

But I have not quite shown why I prize the Montgomery letters. Let us see more closely what they contain, and how they read.

My saying I liked tall flowers that sway in the wind brought this:

> I like every kind. But I like best the flowers I coax into bloom myself, be they tall or small, white or rosy. It seems as if I were taking a hand in creation — giving life to those unsightly bulbs that hide such rainbow possibilities in their cores. Isn't it strange how such ugly things can give birth to such beauty — the old mystery of good, like the white lily, springing out of the muck and mire of evil? Is it possible that evil is necessary to the blossoming of good, just as the dirty clay and foul smelling fertilizers are necessary to the unfolding of those blossoms? There's a theological problem for you!

Here is the poet, stripped of rhyme and metre, though not of fancy's lovely vocabulary, gripping fast the concrete form and fact, then seeing its universal relation.

The letters have many bits of curious, cultured reading. Try this:

> A short time ago, a British magazine ran an interesting series of letters on the idea: If you met the ghost of some famous person, and asked him or her *one* question, what would that question be?
>
> A great many questions were asked, none of which appear in my list below. Half of the writers wished they could meet Shakespeare and ask him if he really did write his plays. Well, there's one question I would like to ask Shakespeare, but 'tis not about his plays. I feel absolutely sure he did write them, and the so-called difficulties stump me not a whit. You can't measure a demi-god with a yardstick.
>
> No, if I met Shakespeare's shade I would ask him, "Why did you leave your wife your second-best bed?" Controversies have raged over this. I should really like to know.

Suppose one met St. Paul and asked him, "What was your thorn in the flesh?"

Or Pilate's wife: "What did you dream of the Nazarene?"

Queen Elizabeth: "Were you, or were you not, secretly married to Robert Dudley?"

Mary Queen of Scots: "Did you know about Darnley's murder?"

Dickens: "Was Edwin Drood really murdered or not?"

Homer: "Was there only one or half a dozen of you?"

Mona Lisa: "What are you smiling at like that?"

Abraham: "Just why did you leave Ur?"

Vashti: "Were you ever sorry you didn't obey Ahasuerus?"

Judas Iscariot: "Why did you really betray Him?"

Yes, I think one could have an interesting time among the ghosts. Can you add any more to the list?

I found it no easy list to extend after St. Paul, Mona Lisa and Iscariot had been taken, though it was fun to try. There are many ghost questions that come to mind, but not many classical cases so specifically puzzling. One would feel like asking any ghost what it feels like to die, but that's too general. I managed to add:

Beethoven: "How did you create those symphonies with a stone-deaf ear?"

Brutus: "Were you never sorry you stabbed Caesar?"

Hamlet: "Which of all the theories about you is right?"

Bishops Ridley and Latimer: "Is it true that in getting burned to death, the nerves are soon seared to insensibility, then easy dying?"

Lucy Gray: "What became of you when you got to the middle of the bridge?

The reply:

As for questioning ghosts, your question for Ridley and Latimer *would* be interesting. I have read that a hot fire paralyzes the nerves at once, and thereafter no pain is felt. This must be true if the stories of triumphant hymn-singing at the stake are reliable. It was the slow fire that was dreadful. I have read that both Ridley and Latimer had little bags of powder hung from their necks to kill them quickly by explosion.

I, too, want to know what happened to Lucy Gray. The awful intriguing mystery of that phrase, "And further there were none," haunted me all through childhood.

I offered the answer I once got from an extra bright pupil: "Lucy evaporated." The next reply told how Lucy's evaporation tickled this Lucy's risibles.

The poetic descriptions that give the Montgomery stories such freshness and cheery imagery make the letters delightful too. A reviewer in the *New York Tribune*, in lingering appreciation, gets at the secret:

> Miss Montgomery at moments has power to recapture and impart the sense of wonder, to present familiar objects in a kind of dawn light as if they were shining new and marvellous.

But just as the describing pen, even though a Carlyle's, must leave it to the camera to bring out the personality behind a face, so the description of an author's style is "without form and void" until we read it. And it takes her Island to liberate L.M. Montgomery's flow of fancies, personifying playfulness, and vital vocabulary.

In a letter I had tried to convey the atmosphere and some immensity of the Canadian prairie, which we were beginning to shred into virgin furrows. Here is the response, October, 1907:

> Though raining now, it was fine this afternoon — oh so fine — sunny and mild as a day in June. I hied me to the woods, away

back to the sun-washed alleys carpeted with fallen gold and glades where the moss is green and vivid yet. The woods are *getting ready* to sleep — they are not *yet* asleep, but are disrobing. There are all kinds of little bed-time conferences and whisperings and good-nights. I can more nearly expect to come face to face with a dryad at this time of the year than any other. They are lurking in every tree trunk. A dozen times I wheeled sharply around, convinced that if I could only turn quick enough I could catch one peeping after me. Oh, keep your great, vast prairies, where never a wood-nymph could hide. I am content with my bosky lanes and the purple, peopled shadows under my firs.

Even so, the sea, to this daughter of the Island, has a mightier spell than the woods. It haunts her, as her line of poetry says, "With a voice of gramarye evermore." Or her letter:

> Three evenings ago I went to the shore. We had had a wild storm of wind and rain the day before, but this evening was clear, cold, with an air of marvellous purity. The sunset was lovely beyond words. I drank its beauty in as I walked down the old shore lane, and my soul was filled with a nameless exhilaration. I seemed borne on the wings of an ecstasy into the seventh heaven.
>
> The shore was clean washed after the storm, and not a wind stirred, but there was a silver surf on, dashing on the sands in a splendid white turmoil. Oh! the glory of that far gaze across the tossing waters, which were the only restless thing in all that vast stillness and peace. It was a moment worth living through weeks of storm and stress for.
>
> There is a great *solitude* about such a shore. The *woods* are never solitary — they are full of whispering, beckoning, friendly life, but the sea is a mighty soul forever moaning of some

unsharable sorrow that shuts itself up into itself for all eterni-
ty. You can never pierce into its great mystery — you can only
wander, awed and spellbound, on the outer fringe of it. The
woods call you with a hundred voices, but the sea has only one
— a mighty voice that drowns your soul with its majestic
music. The woods are human, but the sea is of the company of
the archangels.

Then this daughter of nature, versed in literature, quotes an oracle of
Emerson into living meaning:

> The gods talk in the breath of the wold,
> They talk in the shaken pine,
> And they fill the long reach of the old seashore
> With a dialogue divine.
> And the poet who overhears
> Some random word they say
> Is the fated man of men
> Whom the ages must obey.

I shall never hear that random word; my ear is not attuned to its lofty thun-
der. But I can always *listen*, and haply by times I shall catch the faint, far-off
echoes of it, and even that will flood my soul with its supernal joy.

"But I can always listen" — strikingly like Wordsworth listening to the distant waves: "Listen! The Mighty Being is awake."

I had been wanting to describe to this poetic observer of nature the various
aspects of the Rocky Mountains seventy to a hundred miles west, as seen from
my homestead in various weathers and times of day: the cracked white enamel
of their sunward side the morning after a snowfall; the purple gloom of the shady
side with a rosy sunset behind them; also as seen from a height among them: the
constant shift of sublime scenery from different points and elevations; the thrill
of gazing down thousands of feet into valleys with toy townlets strung along a

looping, silvery river-ribbon; the jumbled chaos of mountain tops seen through waving curtains of rain at moments glorified by sunbeams — all this with enough detail to make it vivid, for she had never seen the Rockies. But that Indian Summer letter of 1907 discouraged me: I felt unable to match her depth.

Of personal anecdotes these letters have plenty. One problem of famous writers is to keep their mail manageable. But again it takes the author to tell it:

> A girl in Australia — may jackals sit on her grandmother's grave — wrote me last fall, and I answered her letter. She published my letter and address in an Australian magazine, something she should not have done without my consent. In midwinter the deluge began. The first wave was eighty-five letters in one day. The local postmaster wanted to know if I were having a wedding anniversary! This continued until May, when they began to dribble off. I have ceased to count them, but there must have been a thousand. My publishers say, "Oh, answer them, if only by a line …" But fancy the work! Do you wonder my poor real correspondents are left out in the cold?

A young fellow in Detroit sent a tidy missive with this address:

> Miss Anne Shirley
> >Care of Miss Martha Cuthbert
> >>Avonlea
> >>>Prince Edward Island
> >>>>Canada
> >>>>>Ontario

Those who know *Anne of Green Gables* and a bit of Canadian geography will be as amused as L.M.M. was. A post office clerk had written across the envelope, "Try Miss Montgomery, Cavendish." Her getting it implies that her Marilla and her Anne enjoyed no mean fame.

Here's a set of gems from my Montgomery letters:

Poetic awe of a night scene:

> Then *the* storm came up, and for half an hour we sat there
> spell-bound, gazing on such a sight as we had never dreamed —
> the great Canadian Falls (Niagara) lying under the ghostly, shim-
> mering, blue-white gleam of almost constant lightning, while
> athwart the mist tore zig-zags of living flame, as if some god were
> amusing himself by hurling thunderbolts into the abyss. No, I
> shall never see the like of that again. But I have seen it once.

Expecting that her publishers would want "that detestable Anne" written
through high-school in a second volume, then through college in a third:

> I'm Anne's slave already. The idea makes me sick. I feel
> like the magician in the eastern story who became the slave of
> the jinn he had himself conjured out of a bottle.

A weird personal experience:

> Mammoth Cave must be terribly full of ghosts. Everyone
> who goes through it must leave something of himself in it, a
> little bit of his soul, his personality, and always wants to go
> back and find it. But does he ever go? I fancy very few peo-
> ple ever revisit Mammoth Cave. It mightn't be safe. *Suppose
> it kept too much of you?*

How free-verse writers, averse to old forms, strain to be original:

> But isn't a beautiful echo more beautiful than the shriek of
> an automobile?

The characterlessness of the "good mixers":

> The only people I ever knew that were worth while were cats who walked by themselves and never pretended to be Maltese if they were tortoise shell.

Immortality of roses:

> Henry Ward Beecher said, "Flowers are the sweetest things God ever made and forgot to put souls into." But I believe He didn't forget. I believe they *have* souls. I have known roses that I expect to meet in Heaven.

Playful allusion:

> After gardening intensely, and cleaning house ferociously for six weeks, I am taking a breathing spell and intend to put off Martha and put on Mary.

Prevention of profanity:

> I never put more than two kinds of flowers together in a bouquet. More would swear at each other.

Kindred spirits:

> I wonder if the spirits of all the pussy folk I have loved will meet me with purrs of gladness at the pearly gates.

L.M. Montgomery prefers the warm individuality of the human hand to the cold Roman universality of the typewriter. In the forty years of this literary exchange she never typed me a letter. A typed letter from her would have been the high handshake. No, the handwriting of the well-seasoned correspondent is no matter for an encroaching machine to profane, even when, as in this case, the writing is hard to read; for slow reading allows fond lingering on the lines.

What, then, in sum and substance, are the merits of these letters? Their style is so facile and natural that you forget it isn't conversation. There is open sincerity, clear conviction, free familiarity and a playful originality of fancy, with freshness of diction; live subject matter, personal and general, made still more interesting by genial comment; poetic feeling that brings melody and rhythm into the sentences; stimulating thought, strengthened or adorned with bits from lore and legend; and a courteous patience that brought ample replies to my more commonplace news and less adventurous lay experience.

And what were her last words to me? — "We've had a good friendship in our own way," she wrote, explaining that a "hypo" enabled her to hold a pen for a few moments.

This correspondence has made me fonder of the great letters of the masters: Samuel Johnson, Shelley, Cowper, Horace Walpole, Goethe, Lincoln, Carlyle and his wife Jane, for a few; and I still intend to nibble at Madame de Sevigné.

Notes

1   Marjorie MacMurchy was a friend of Maud's and lived in Toronto. Maud would visit her in Toronto, staying several days at her home, and the two friends attended plays and social events together. Ms. MacMurchy is mentioned several times in Montgomery's journals and is also featured in a photo. She wrote several articles about her friend L.M. Montgomery. Two photos originally accompanied this article: one was of the Campbell home in Park Corner where Maud and Ewan were married; the other was of Chester with a cat. Both were taken by L.M. Montgomery, who must have given them to Miss MacMurchy.

2   L.M. Montgomery was born at Clifton (now known as New London) on November 30, 1874.

3   Montgomery always spelled her Macneill relatives' names with a small *n*, rather than the large *N* used here.

4   Montgomery travelled to Prince Albert in what is now Saskatchewan (it was part of the North West Territories at the time) in August 1890, when she was fifteen years old.

5   When Montgomery arrived in Prince Albert, her father and stepmother had one child, two-year-old Kate. During the year L.M. Montgomery was there, her stepmother gave birth to her second child, Bruce, on February 1, 1891. Two more siblings were born after L.M. Montgomery left Prince Albert: Ila and Carl.

6   Maud attended Dalhousie University in Halifax from 1895 to 1896, and was employed as a journalist at the *Halifax Daily Echo* from 1901 to 1902.

7   Montgomery's grandfather, Alexander Macneill, died March 6, 1898, while she was in Lower Bedeque, working as a teacher. She gave up her teaching job to stay at home and care for her grandmother.

8   By the time *Anne of Green Gables* was published in 1908, Montgomery was making enough to live on from the stories and poems she sold to major

Canadian and American publications, including well-known ones such as *Ladies Home Journal, Good Housekeeping,* and *Canadian Magazine.*

9   After the success of *Anne of Green Gables,* her publisher, L.C. Page Company, asked Montgomery to write a sequel immediately; this would be *Anne of Avonlea.* In 1909 the company decided they wanted Montgomery to rewrite and lengthen a serial of hers (*Una of the Garden*) that had recently been published in a magazine. It became her third book, *Kilmeny of the Orchard.*

10 The story of this cat, named Daffy, is documented in a children's book — *Lucy Maud and the Cavendish Cat* — published in 1997 by Tundra Books.

11 This jug became the focus of a book written by Montgomery entitled *A Tangled Web,* published in 1931.

12 Webb.

13 "Letter bills" are the sheets of paper for use in mail bags, approximately the length of a sheet of lady's writing paper. (This is an original footnote from the original article.)

14 This was not a newspaper clipping. L.M. Montgomery got this idea from Rachel and Pierce Macneill, who lived on a neighbouring farm. They'd asked for an orphan boy to be sent to them, but instead received a girl. Montgomery wrote the idea in her notebook for future use as a story.

15 L.M. Montgomery received a letter from Mark Twain's secretary, I.V. Lyon, dated October 3, 1908, who wrote: "Mr. Clemens directs me to thank you for your charming book and says I may quote to you from his letter to Francis Wilson about it: 'In "Anne of Green Gables" you will find the dearest and most moving and delightful child since the immortal Alice.'"

16 Reverend Cowan misspells "Anne" as "Ann" throughout this article. This has been corrected here. All other spelling remains as it appeared in the original article.

17 Montgomery wrote the manuscript and sent it to several publishers. They all rejected it, and discouraged, she put it away. In 1907, she took it out again, thinking that perhaps she would shorten it and send it out to magazines. However, after reading it again, she decided to give it one more

chance and sent it to L.C. Page of Boston. They accepted it and it was published in 1908.

18 Ephraim Weber was a correspondent of Maud's from 1902 to her death in 1942. At one point, he suggested that he could write her biography if she were to die first, but Maud nixed the idea. Instead, Mr. Weber wrote this article for the *Dalhousie Review* following her death.